Parenting

Roman Espejo, Book Editor

GREENHAVEN PRESS
A part of Gale, Cengage Learning

Detroit • New York • San Francisco • New Haven, Conn • Waterville, Maine • London

GALE
CENGAGE Learning

Elizabeth Des Chenes, *Director, Publishing Solutions*

For more information, contact:
Greenhaven Press
27500 Drake Rd.
Farmington Hills, MI 48331-3535
Or you can visit our Internet site at gale.cengage.com

Articles in Greenhaven Press anthologies are often edited for length to meet page requirements. In addition, original titles of these works are changed to clearly present the main thesis and to explicitly indicate the author's opinion. Every effort is made to ensure that Greenhaven Press accurately reflects the original intent of the authors. Every effort has been made to trace the owners of copyrighted material.

LIBRARY OF CONGRESS CATALOGING-IN-PUBLICATION DATA

Parenting / Roman Espejo, book editor.
p. cm. -- (Opposing viewpoints)
Includes bibliographical references and index.
ISBN 978-0-7377-6336-2 (hbk.) -- ISBN 978-0-7377-6337-9 (pbk.)
1. Parents--United States. 2. Parenthood--United States. 3. Parent and child (Law)--United States. I. Espejo, Roman, 1977-
HQ755.8.P3787 2013
649'.1--dc23

2012036911

Printed in the United States of America
1 2 3 4 5   17 16 15 14 13

Contents

Why Consider Opposing Viewpoints?

> *"The only way in which a human being can make some approach to knowing the whole of a subject is by hearing what can be said about it by persons of every variety of opinion and studying all modes in which it can be looked at by every character of mind. No wise man ever acquired his wisdom in any mode but this."*
>
> *John Stuart Mill*

In our media-intensive culture it is not difficult to find differing opinions. Thousands of newspapers and magazines and dozens of radio and television talk shows resound with differing points of view. The difficulty lies in deciding which opinion to agree with and which "experts" seem the most credible. The more inundated we become with differing opinions and claims, the more essential it is to hone critical reading and thinking skills to evaluate these ideas. Opposing Viewpoints books address this problem directly by presenting stimulating debates that can be used to enhance and teach these skills. The varied opinions contained in each book examine many different aspects of a single issue. While examining these conveniently edited opposing views, readers can develop critical thinking skills such as the ability to compare and contrast authors' credibility, facts, argumentation styles, use of persuasive techniques, and other stylistic tools. In short, the Opposing Viewpoints Series is an ideal way to attain the higher-level thinking and reading skills so essential in a culture of diverse and contradictory opinions.

In addition to providing a tool for critical thinking, Opposing Viewpoints books challenge readers to question their own strongly held opinions and assumptions. Most people form their opinions on the basis of upbringing, peer pressure, and personal, cultural, or professional bias. By reading carefully balanced opposing views, readers must directly confront new ideas as well as the opinions of those with whom they disagree. This is not to argue simplistically that everyone who reads opposing views will—or should—change his or her opinion. Instead, the series enhances readers' understanding of their own views by encouraging confrontation with opposing ideas. Careful examination of others' views can lead to the readers' understanding of the logical inconsistencies in their own opinions, perspective on why they hold an opinion, and the consideration of the possibility that their opinion requires further evaluation.

Evaluating Other Opinions

To ensure that this type of examination occurs, Opposing Viewpoints books present all types of opinions. Prominent spokespeople on different sides of each issue as well as well-known professionals from many disciplines challenge the reader. An additional goal of the series is to provide a forum for other, less known, or even unpopular viewpoints. The opinion of an ordinary person who has had to make the decision to cut off life support from a terminally ill relative, for example, may be just as valuable and provide just as much insight as a medical ethicist's professional opinion. The editors have two additional purposes in including these less known views. One, the editors encourage readers to respect others' opinions—even when not enhanced by professional credibility. It is only by reading or listening to and objectively evaluating others' ideas that one can determine whether they are worthy of consideration. Two, the inclusion of such viewpoints encourages the important critical thinking skill of objectively evaluating an author's credentials and bias. This evaluation will illuminate an author's reasons for taking a particular stance on an issue and will aid in readers' evaluation of the author's ideas.

It is our hope that these books will give readers a deeper understanding of the issues debated and an appreciation of the complexity of even seemingly simple issues when good and honest people disagree. This awareness is particularly important in a democratic society such as ours in which people enter into public debate to determine the common good. Those with whom one disagrees should not be regarded as enemies but rather as people whose views deserve careful examination and may shed light on one's own.

Thomas Jefferson once said that "difference of opinion leads to inquiry, and inquiry to truth." Jefferson, a broadly educated man, argued that "if a nation expects to be ignorant and free . . . it expects what never was and never will be." As individuals and as a nation, it is imperative that we consider the opinions of others and examine them with skill and discernment. The Opposing Viewpoints series is intended to help readers achieve this goal.

David L. Bender and Bruno Leone,
Founders

Introduction

> *"The concept of attachment parenting holds tremendous power—in the process of raising our children, we raise ourselves."*
>
> *—Barbara Nicholson, coauthor of* Attached at the Heart: 8 Proven Parenting Principles for Raising Connected and Compassionate Children

> *"With all of its demands, the naturalist ideal of [attachment parenting] means that it takes a woman as much time and energy to raise two children as our grandmothers spent raising four."*
>
> *—Elisabeth Badinter, author of* The Conflict: How Modern Motherhood Undermines the Status of Women

In 2012 actress and neuroscientist Mayim Bialik attracted national attention to attachment parenting with her book, *Beyond the Sling: A Real-Life Guide to Raising Confident, Loving Children the Attachment Parenting Way*. Bialik proposes that attachment parenting fosters independence in children while enhancing connections with their mothers and fathers. "Securely attached children separate from their parents easily, react well when reunited with them, seek out their parents for comfort and security, and prefer their parents to strangers," writes the mother of two. Furthermore, parents instinctively know the majority of what makes good parenting, Bialik contends, and today's practices complicate the basics of teaching a child to sleep, eat, and learn. "I propose that we, for the most part, need very little of this kind of help in these matters," she continues. "By understanding the basic theories of attachment and infant development . . . and by trusting that everything a baby needs is communicated honestly, simply, and without malice or manipulation, we can truly be the parents that nature intends us to be."

According to Attachment Parenting International (API), the parenting style, named by pediatrician William Sears, follows eight principles from pregnancy through early childhood:

- Preparation for Pregnancy, Birth, and Parenting
- Feed with Love and Respect
- Respond with Sensitivity
- Use Nurturing Touch
- Ensure Safe Sleep, Physically and Emotionally
- Provide Consistent Loving Care
- Practice Positive Discipline
- Strive for Balance in Personal and Family Life

The formation and fostering of strong bonds between parent and child is at the core of attachment parenting, states API. "In many ways, it is a return to the instinctual behaviors of our ancestors," API states on its website. Indeed, in her view as a neurologist, Bialik declares in *Beyond the Sling* that these principles are based on evolution. "They foster brain development, promote healthy and secure attachment, and produce relationships that are scientifically proven to be sound in terms of infant health, psychological achievement, and the ability to truly thrive," she explains.

Nonetheless, some of the principles of attachment parenting are scrutinized. For instance, its approach includes bed sharing, or having the baby or child sleep with the parents in the same bed, to allow for nursing and immediate care at all hours. "Knowing that my babies were right next to me at night allowed me to rest knowing that I could tell if they were too hot, too cold, not breathing right—whatever," Bialik says in *Beyond the Sling*. But the American Academy of Pediatrics (AAP), the largest pediatric organization in the country, discourages bed sharing due to the risk of sudden infant death syndrome (SIDS), when a baby unexpectedly dies in sleep during the first year of life. Published in 2012, a meta-analysis of eleven studies conducted by researchers at Germany's Institute of Legal Medicine and Forensic Sciences found that babies who slept in the same beds as their parents were three times more likely to die of SIDS. Still, proponents of bed sharing counter such findings. William Sears points out that where the practice is most common, the rates of SIDS are the lowest. "While there could be many other factors contributing to the lower incidence of SIDS in these cultures, all the population studies I've seen have come to the same conclusion: Safe co-sleeping lowers the SIDS risk," he contends. Also, Sears maintains, bed sharing can promote "nighttime harmony" in the sleep arousal patterns of mothers and babies, reducing the chance of SIDS. "The co-sleeping mom is more likely to subconsciously sense if her baby's health is in danger and wake up," he suggests.

The principle of feeding in attachment parenting is also a divisive issue. In May 2012, a *Time* magazine cover featuring a mother breast-feeding her almost four-year-old son for a story on the parenting approach generated controversy. In its 2011 breast-feeding report card, the Centers for Disease Control and Prevention reported that 81.9 percent of infants were ever breast-fed, 46.2 percent were breast-fed exclusively through three months, and 25.5 percent were breast-fed exclusively through six months. It is generally recommended that children are breast-fed until twenty-four months, but it's common for mothers to cease nursing at twelve months. API claims that breast-feeding is superior to all other methods of feeding, and the organization supports extending it longer. "Breast-feeding continues to be normal and important nutritionally, immunologically, and emotionally beyond one year," states API. API also views weaning as a "cooperative process between mother and baby" that should be initiated when the child shows cues of wanting to wean. On the other hand, some doubt that nursing has benefits over bottle-feeding. "We have clear indications that breast-feeding helps prevent an extra incident of gastrointestinal illness in some kids—an unpleasant few days of diarrhea or vomiting, but rarely life-threatening in developed countries. We have murky correlations with a whole bunch of long-term conditions," states journalist Hanna Rosin in an April 2009 article in the *Atlantic.* Furthermore, Rosin persists in an article in *Slate* in March 2012 that attachment parenting adds the pressure that "it's not just enough to breast-feed, but one has to experience 'breast-feeding induced maternal nirvana.'"

In fact, the concept of attachment parenting itself is criticized. Novelist and essayist Erica Jong argues that it is far from natural and promotes oppressive expectations of mothering. "Attachment parenting, especially when combined with environmental correctness, has encouraged female victimization. Women feel not only that they must be ever-present for their children but also that they must breast-feed, make their own baby food, and eschew disposable diapers," she writes in the *Wall Street Journal.* Jong is also skeptical of what it teaches children about relationships and identity. "What does attachment parenting tell daughters about how big their dreams should be? How does it teach sons not to expect women to cater to their every whim? How does it teach any child that the world does not revolve around him or her?" she asks.

Attachment parenting is one of the forms and ways to raise children that are practiced—and contested—in modern society; other debatable parenting topics range from corporal punishment to same-sex couples raising a family. *Opposing Viewpoints: Parenting* explores these topics and others in the following chapters: How Should Parents Discipline Their Children?, Do Some Forms of Parenting Put Children at a Disadvantage?, and Are Parents Liable for Their Children's Actions? The varied and conflicting positions and arguments selected for this volume reflect the complexities of parenthood and how parents' actions, behaviors, and parenting styles affect their children.

How Should Parents Discipline Their Children?

Chapter Preface

In 2010 the C.S. Mott Children's Hospital National Poll on Children's Health reported that physical punishment is not the first form of discipline for parents with children. Twenty-two percent of parents were very likely to spank their children, and 10 percent responded that they used paddling. In contrast, 88 percent of parents were very likely to explain or try reasoning with their children, 70 percent revoked privileges or something their children enjoy, and 59 percent resorted to grounding or placing their children in time-out. Using more than one of these methods was also very likely among many parents.

Interestingly, the poll also found the likelihood of parents to spank their children varied geographically: 31 percent in the West, 20 percent in the South, 16 percent in the Midwest, and 6 percent in the Northeast. "These regional differences are a reminder that parents' choices of discipline are rooted in strong cultural traditions," explains Matthew Davis, associate professor of pediatrics and communicable diseases at the University of Michigan Medical School. "Even as national trends have shifted away from physical to verbal discipline," he continues, "there are likely community cues and informal networks of parents and grandparents that influence how parents discipline their kids."

It is frequently upheld, for example, that African Americans are more likely to use corporal punishment on their children because it is a part of their culture. "Many blacks have no tolerance for the prevalence of 'talking back,' public tantrums, and authoritativeness displayed by nonblack children and believe that the absence of spanking induces such behavior," asserts parenting and culture columnist LaShaun Williams in the *New York Times*. "It's not uncommon to hear parents of black children being raised in affluent white communities reiterate their blackness in justifying spanking their kids as a cultural reminder of who they are," she maintains. Reactions to Williams's position among readers were split. One commentator said that being spanked was never a source of resentment because "we always understood that it was a consequence of our own actions," while another argued that Williams must consider that getting hit by parents "makes the world a different place for black children." In the following chapter, the authors examine the effectiveness and appropriateness of how parents punish and discipline their sons and daughters.

VIEWPOINT 

"The proper use of corporal punishment is in the best interest of children."

Corporal Punishment Is Effective

James Dobson

Founder of traditional values organization Focus on the Family, James Dobson is a psychologist and author of The New Strong-Willed Child. *In the following viewpoint excerpted from that book, Dobson advocates the use of corporal punishment to discipline children and differentiates it from child abuse and destructive parenting. He asserts that appropriate spanking is necessary when a child understands what actions to take and refuses to yield to parental authority; he also claims that it is the most effective way to change a child's attitude. In addition, Dobson highly recommends the option of corporal punishment for tough-minded kids to prevent both children and parents from losing control in tense confrontations.*

As you read, consider the following questions:

1. According to Dobson, how is it possible to use corporal punishment wrongly and create an aggressive child?

James Dobson, "Corporal Punishment & the Strong-Willed Child," *The New Strong-Willed Child*, Tyndale House Publishers, Inc., 2007.

2. Instead of creating aggression in children, how does corporal punishment help them, in Dobson's view?
3. How does managing children only by talking and reasoning during confrontations affect parents, as maintained by Dobson?

Given the delicate relationship between parents and their children and the rising incidence of physical and emotional assaults on boys and girls, the last thing I want to do is to provide a rationalization or justification for anything that could hurt them. Let me say it once more: I don't believe in harsh, oppressive, demeaning discipline, even when it is well-intentioned. Such destructive parenting is antithetical to everything I believe and stand for. At the risk of sounding self-serving, let me say that among the honors and awards I have received through the years, the one I value most is a bronze statue of a small boy and girl. The arm of one of the children is outstretched as though reaching for the loving hand of an adult. The inscription on the base of the statue, given by an organization dedicated to the prevention of child abuse, designated me as "The Children's Friend" in that year.

Considering this lifelong commitment to the welfare of children, why would I recommend corporal punishment as a management tool? It is a very good question, especially in view of the many articles and editorials appearing in the media these days that resoundingly condemn its use. Convincing the public that corporal punishment is universally harmful has become an unrelenting crusade within certain elements of the liberal media. I believe their efforts have been terribly misguided.

I would be quick to acknowledge that corporal punishment *can* be harmful when used wrongly. It *is* possible ... even easy ... to create an aggressive child who has observed violent episodes at home. If he is routinely beaten by parents, or if he witnesses physical violence between angry adults, the child will not fail to notice how the game is played. Thus, corporal punishment that is not administered according to very carefully thought-out guidelines has the potential to become dangerous. Parenthood does not give the right to slap and intimidate a child because Dad had a bad day or Mom is in a lousy mood. It is this kind of unjust discipline that causes some well-meaning authorities to reject corporal punishment altogether.

A Desperately Needed Resolution to Disobedience

Just because a useful technique can be used wrongly, however, is no reason to reject it altogether. Many children desperately need this resolution to their disobedience. In those situations when the child fully understands what he is being asked to do or not to do but refuses to yield to adult leadership, an appropriate spanking is the shortest and most effective route to an attitude adjustment. When he lowers his head, clenches his fists, and makes it clear he is going for broke, justice must speak swiftly and eloquently. This response does not create aggression in children, but it does help them control their impulses and live in harmony with various forms of benevolent authority throughout life.

There is another reason I believe the proper use of corporal punishment is in the best interest of children. Strong-willed boys and girls can be terribly irritating to their parents, as we all know. Most of them have figured out how to press all the right (or wrong) buttons to make their moms and dads absolutely furious. One father said that nothing in his adult experience could make him more angry than the rebellious behavior of his ten-year-old son, day after day. Given that kind of volatile interaction, I am convinced that a determined, hard-nosed kid in the hands of an immature or emotionally unstable parent is a recipe for disaster. The likelihood of physical damage to that youngster is enormous, and it becomes even greater if the parents have been stripped of the ability to control challenging behavior before it gets out of hand.

When permissive advice-givers convince moms and dads that they can, and must, manage their children by talking and reasoning during nose-to-nose confrontations, the parents get more and more frustrated as the misbehavior intensifies. Eventually, too many of them blow up, and when they do, anything can happen. I am convinced that child abuse often emerges from that scenario in one way or another. How much better, and safer, it is for moms and dads to administer a judicious and carefully measured spanking to a child (or even a well-timed swat or two), before she and her parents are both out of control. It is even more advantageous for a savvy strong-willed child to know that spanking is an option, leading him to back off before he goes too far. By depriving parents of this possibility, the well-meaning counselors and psychologists inadvertently set up tough-minded kids for disaster at home. . . .

An Example of Correct Corporal Punishment

Here's an example of corporal punishment administered correctly and with the desired result. It was relayed to me by a father, William Jarnagin, a certified public accountant, who wrote me the following letter. It speaks volumes about the proper approach to parent-child relationships:

> *Dear Dr. Dobson:*
>
> *This is a note of thanks for your work in strengthening the American family. My wife and I have recently read four of your books and we have profited very much from them.*
>
> *Please permit me to relate a recent experience with our six-year-old son, David. Last Friday night, my wife, Becky, told him to pick up some orange peelings he had left on the carpet,*

Steve Kelley Editorial Cartoon used with permission of Steve Kelley and Creators Syndicate.

which he knows is a "no-no." He failed to respond, and as a result received one slap on his behind, whereupon he began an obviously defiant temper tantrum.

Since I had observed the whole episode, I then called for my paddle and applied it appropriately, saw to it that he picked up and properly disposed of the orange peelings, and sent him straight to bed, since it was already past his bedtime. After a few minutes, when his emotions had had a chance to settle down, I went to his room and explained that God had instructed all parents who truly love their children to properly discipline them, etc., and that we truly love him and therefore would not permit such defiant behavior.

The next morning, after I had gone to work, David presented his mother with the following letter, together with a little stack of ten pennies:

From David and Deborah

To Mom and Dad

Ross Dr. 3d house

Sellmer, Tennasse

39718

Dear Mom and Dad here is 10 Cints for Pattelling me when I really neded and that gos for Deborah to I love you

Love yur son David and yur Doter Deborah

Oh, incidentally, Deborah is our one-year-old daughter whose adoption should be final sometime in June.

Keep up your good work and may God bless you.

Sincerely,

William H. Jarnagin

Mr. William Jarnagin understands the appropriate response of a father to a child's defiance. It is neither harsh nor insulting nor dangerous nor whimsical. Rather, it represents the firm but loving discipline that is required for the best interest of the child. How fortunate is the boy or girl whose father and mother still comprehend that timeless concept.

VIEWPOINT 

"The line between acceptable corporal punishment and dangerous physical abuse is usually drawn in the sand on a blustery day; there are no guidelines."

Corporal Punishment Is Ineffective and Abusive

Melanie Barwick

Melanie Barwick is a psychologist and health systems scientist in the Community Health Systems Resource Group at SickKids in Toronto, Canada. In the following viewpoint, she opposes corporal punishment to discipline children. Although such punishment results in immediate compliance, Barwick maintains that children must be taught to control their behavior with internalized morals and values—not external physical threats—for healthy socialization. Moreover, harsh punishment is associated with depression and stress in adolescence, she states, and coercive parenting leads to increased feelings of helplessness and humiliation among children. Barwick adds that children's brains are still developing, and misbehavior is not always intentional but linked to a lack of maturity, understanding, or impulse control.

Melanie Barwick, "Parenting: The Line Between Punishment and Abuse," CBC News, June 24, 2008.

As you read, consider the following questions:

1. What is Barwick's view of a parent or caregiver who does not mean to cause harm with corporal punishment?
2. In the author's view, how can children's knowledge of the right way to behave be enhanced?
3. What does physical punishment communicate to children, as stated by the author?

Section 43 of Canada's criminal code allows parents, teachers and caregivers to use reasonable force to discipline a child and correct their behaviour. Bill S-209, which needs House [of Commons] approval to be made into law, proposes to eliminate section 43 of Canada's criminal code and give adults the right to physically discipline children between the ages of two and 12 [the bill has not been passed].

The code calls to mind several questions:

- How were these age parameters chosen?
- Is there something about being younger than two or older than 12 that suggests greater harm from physical punishment will befall these children as compared to children three to 11?
- Where do we draw the line in disciplining our children and what right does the government have to legislate parenting or caregiving style?
- How do you balance a parent's right to parent and a kid's right not to be abused?

The purpose of the bill, according to Liberal senator Céline Hervieux-Payette, who introduced it, is "to send a signal, so that people who use violence in a repeated way will no longer feel protected.... It is not to arrest everyone who gives their child a tap on the arm." The bill was amended to allow parents and caregivers to use force in very specific situations—such as when a caregiver wants to immediately stop a child from doing something dangerous that could cause serious harm, presumably to him or herself or to others.

In the same vein, a Quebec court recently ruled that a father didn't have the right to punish his 12-year-old daughter by barring her from a school trip after he grounded her for risky behaviour—posting pictures of herself on an Internet dating service.

Two Important Characteristics

Two important characteristics set these stories apart.

The first is that while one situation focuses on physical punishment, also known as corporal punishment, the other deals with nonphysical discipline. Corporal punishment is the use of physical force with the intent of causing a child to experience pain but not injury for the purposes of correction or control of the child's behaviour.

The line between acceptable corporal punishment and dangerous physical abuse is usually drawn in the sand on a blustery day; there are no guidelines. Physical abuse is the infliction of physical injury through punching, kicking, beating, biting, burning, shaking or otherwise harming a child.

Whether a parent or caregiver did not intend to cause harm doesn't make it more acceptable. In the end, it's about one person asserting power over another and there's nothing healthy in that dynamic.

The second important consideration is the difference between children behaving badly and those whose behaviour places them at risk or in harm's way. Children who act impulsively or who take risks are often the focus of parental discipline.

Let's tackle physical punishment first and ask, is hitting detrimental to children? The comments posted by a great many readers in reference to the anti-spanking bill suggest that physical punishment has been the personal experience of many adults during their own childhood. The common sentiment is that it can't be so bad if they turned out OK.

Recognizing that our beliefs and attitudes shape our behaviour in whatever we do, including parenting and discipline, it is not surprising that this practice continues to be used.

I wonder if the same people who hold this view of physical punishment also place importance on the value of research evidence as it relates to health care, for instance.

Those battling illness would like to receive medical care that is based on the best scientific evidence, as is our right. So why shouldn't parenting practices be subject to the same evidence-based criteria? What *does* the research say about the effectiveness and outcomes of physical punishment of children?

Should Canada step in to adopt policies or laws that prohibit parents from using corporal punishment as a means of discipline, as have Austria, Croatia, Cyprus, Denmark, Finland, Germany, Israel, Italy, Latvia, Norway, and Sweden? Or should we align ourselves with the United States, where 94% of parents report spanking their children by the time they are three or four years of age?

This is a complex issue that has been examined in different cultures, genders, and family situations. Most of the research is not designed to address issues of causality—whether physical punishment *causes* certain outcomes. Rather, it looks at explaining how physical punishment is associated or *linked* with children's outcomes.

Much of the research on parents' use of corporal punishment has found it to be associated with negative outcomes. Immediate compliance is a notable exception, however. We know from laboratory research on learning that corporal punishment is indeed effective in getting people to be compliant in the short term; it is effective at stopping bad behaviour immediately.

Internalizing Socially Appropriate Ways of Behaving

But is this our only goal?

While immediate compliance is often what we're after when we discipline, parents need to promote children's ability to control their behaviour using internal controls because these are skills that are more important to long-term socialization.

We want children to behave well not because they don't want to get hit, an external motivator, but because they have internalized socially appropriate ways of behaving. Knowing what the right way to behave is on the inside is enhanced by parental discipline strategies that use minimal parental power, promote choice and autonomy, and provide explanations for desirable behaviours.

Several research reviews have concluded that corporal punishment is associated with increases in children's aggressive behaviour. Parents may be effectively stopping misbehaviour but they are also modeling aggression.

Corporal punishment has also been linked to criminal and antisocial behaviours, likely because corporal punishment does not facilitate children's internalization of morals and values. There is also research on the negative effects of corporal punishment on parent-child relationships, which can evoke feelings of fear, anxiety and anger in children.

Harsh punishment has been linked to depression and distress in adolescence, and coercive parenting techniques have been associated with increases in feelings of humiliation and helplessness. The upshot seems to be that physical punishment may stop bad behaviour in its tracks but it will do noth-

A Symptom of Poor Behavior Management

Spanking is actually a symptom of poor behavior management. It is something parents default to when they do not have knowledge of more sophisticated and effective, positive parenting techniques. The belief that spanking is equivalent to good parenting and good discipline is a myth. I can guarantee that whatever your parenting goals are, they can be achieved much better without spanking. As a matter of fact, spanking will only serve to strongly *interfere* with any possible desirable parenting goals you may have. It will create many more problems than it will ever solve! The vast body of behavioral science research concluding that spanking is harmful to the development of children is one of the best-kept secrets in child psychology.

Michael J. Marshall, Why Spanking Doesn't Work: Stopping This Bad Habit and Getting the Upper Hand on Effective Discipline. *Springville, UT: Bonneville Books, 2002.*

ing to ensure healthy child development, positive parent-child relationships, or healthy social skills for success in life.

What about risk-taking behaviour? What are our rights to discipline when children act in ways that attract harm or danger? Slapping a child's hand away from a burning flame, pulling a child from oncoming traffic, or using nonphysical discipline when children place themselves in harm's way—say by posting pictures on the web—are all behaviours that come instinctively to most parents. They are essentially behaviours driven by our protective instincts. When it comes to understanding children's behaviour, it is helpful to know something about how brain development plays a role in how kids behave.

A Developmental View

These are *developing* children we are talking about. We should not automatically attribute their misbehaviour as intentional for it may at times be related to impulsivity, lack of understanding, or immaturity in how kids think about the world (cognitive immaturity). Sometimes, it's a case of "their brain made them do it."

Case in point: Some researchers are looking at how the brain may account for the risky behaviours and poor decisions that plague adolescence. According to AboutKidsHealth, if we are to understand the problems of teenage behaviour, it is important to look at development over a long period of time instead of examining "snapshots" of teenage decision making.

When we take this developmental view, we see that behaviour does not change in a straight line or linear manner from childhood through to adulthood. The peak of inappropriate and emotional behaviour during adolescence is described as risky and impulsive, often the types of behaviours that get kids into trouble with their parents. Impulsivity, or lack of cognitive control, is not the same thing as risk taking; they are controlled by two separate regions in the brain. More importantly, each region matures according to a different timetable.

AboutKidsHealth goes on to say that risky behaviour does not improve consistently and evenly from childhood through adulthood, but rather peaks in the teenage years, revealing an issue that is unique to adolescence. In some cases, teenagers make significantly poorer decisions than children half their age.

What accounts for this? Well, a part of the brain called the limbic system for one thing. Researchers have shown that risk taking is linked to this deep part of the brain, which is involved with judging incentives and emotional information. Brain imaging shows that risk taking and processing emotional information intensifies activity in the limbic system—

this part of the brain "lights up" on MRI [magnetic resonance imaging] screening when it gets activated, and this intensification is exaggerated during the teen years.

This means that when a risky choice has a strong emotional incentive, such as winning the admiration of peers, the limbic system is strongly activated by the emotional heft of the situation. The emotional, incentive-driven limbic system wins over the immature prefrontal control system—and a risky choice is made.

And so, it isn't always about intentionally being disobedient. Admittedly, the brain is not the only cause of misbehaviour, but as Ross Hetherington, director of AboutKidsHealth, explains, "understanding the neurobiological basis of this disconnection between knowing what is right and doing what is wrong should help parents be patient with the foibles of the typical teenager."

Perhaps it is a simplistic view but, in the end, hitting children to control their behaviour is just not a good thing when you consider the science, and it may very soon be an unwise choice from a legal standpoint.

Famed psychologist B.F. Skinner clearly demonstrated the power both positive and negative reinforcement have to shape behaviour. However, we have more positive and healthy ways to promote pro-social and compliant behaviour in human beings, children and adults alike. Learning to parent positively in an age-appropriate manner may go a long way to preventing the escalation of conflict and misbehaviour that elicits physical punishment.

Make no mistake, physical punishment may very well communicate "stop this immediately," but it also communicates "I am bigger and stronger than you, which means I have power over you and can hurt you if you do not do or act as I say."

We have policies in place that most people support to guard against bullying in school, in the workplace (because adults don't like being hit, yelled at, or belittled, either), and we have laws that protect us from assault and violence. These laws are accepted as warranted and useful. We also have laws in place to guard animals from abusive behaviour.

It is only fitting then that we provide our children the same rights and pay them the same respect we do the household dog and cat.

VIEWPOINT 

"Being able to distinguish between reasonable corporal punishment and maltreatment—whether this is formally denominated abuse or neglect—is critical."

The Legal Distinction Between Corporal Punishment and Abuse Must Be Defined

Doriane Lambelet Coleman, Kenneth A. Dodge, and Sarah Keeton Campbell

In the following viewpoint, Doriane Lambelet Coleman, Kenneth A. Dodge, and Sarah Keeton Campbell argue that the existing legal concepts of corporal punishment and child abuse are inadequate. According to them, states do not have sufficient definitions for "reasonable corporal punishment" and "maltreatment" or have a system of categorizing accidental and non-accidental injuries to minors. The vagueness of abuse definitions, the authors contend, results in the failed fulfillment of laws, inconsistent case outcomes, and the risk of incorrectly identifying or dismissing findings of maltreatment. Therefore, they advocate a

Doriane Lambelet Coleman, Kenneth A. Dodge, and Sarah Keeton Campbell, "Where and How to Draw the Line Between Reasonable Corporal Punishment and Abuse," *Law and Contemporary Problems*, vol. 73, no. 107, 2010, pp. 107–113. Duke University Law.

standard based on the concept of functional impairment to distinguish between reasonable corporal punishment and child abuse. Coleman is a law professor at Duke Law School. Dodge is the William McDougall Professor of Public Policy, a psychology and neuroscience professor, and the director of the Center for Child and Family Policy at Duke University. Campbell is an attorney based in Washington, DC.

As you read, consider the following questions:

1. What is decision making about child injury cases based on without clear definitions of punishment and abuse, as claimed by the authors?
2. In the authors' opinion, why is it difficult to create precise statutory language for child abuse in the United States?
3. Why do authors advocate the functional impairment standard to evaluate corporal punishment and child abuse?

Non-accidental physical injuries children suffer at the hands of their parents occur along a continuum that ranges from mild to severe. At the outer edges of this continuum, one might find, on the one hand, a slight swat to the buttocks, and on the other, a brutal beating. In the United States, the normative consensus appears to be that outsiders to the family are appropriately concerned only when the physical injury at issue causes serious harm; any injury short of a serious one is exclusively "family business."

Consistent with this consensus, all states' laws permit the use of "reasonable" corporal punishment; simultaneously, they all prohibit non-accidentally inflicted serious injury. The latter is generally denominated abuse, although some states classify milder but still impermissible injuries as neglect, or simply "inappropriate discipline." Thus, being able to distinguish between reasonable corporal punishment and maltreatment—

whether this is formally denominated abuse or neglect—is critical for the relevant actors: parents who use corporal punishment as a disciplinary tool, Child Protective Services (CPS) staff who are required by statute to intervene in the family to protect children subject to or at risk of abuse, and courts adjudicating issues arising in connection with these cases. The integrity of the distinction and of the methodology employed to make it is also critical for a society that is prominently committed to both family autonomy and child welfare, and in particular to protecting the integrity of the family when it promotes (or at least does not harm) child welfare, and to intervening in the family when it fails in its related obligations.

Insufficient Definitions and Inconsistent Outcomes

Unfortunately, few if any states have sufficiently defined the relevant terms "reasonable corporal punishment" or "maltreatment" (abuse or neglect) to consistently guide the relevant actors (those in a single system) in their exercises of discretion; nor have they established a coherent methodology for sorting injuries along the continuum of non-accidental physical injuries. That administrative regulations and policies promulgated by state and local CPS departments often narrow agency discretion helps CPS itself to be more consistent and may help families know what to expect when they are dealing with CPS. But because appellate courts do not appear to give much deference to agency interpretations of the statutory definitions, these regulations and policies do little to guide the courts' own exercise of discretion. Moreover, to the extent that the law in statutes and judicial opinions is either less precise or even different from the law as it is applied by CPS, the public and parents are inevitably confused or misled. As a result, decision making about whether an injury or incident remains in the realm of family business or has crossed the line into the impermissible varies, reflecting a multiplicity of purely personal viewpoints, religious and political ideologies, and academic or disciplinary training and requirements. In turn, institutional treatment of and outcomes for children and families are often inconsistent.

The status quo has been defended or at least explained on several grounds. The vagueness of abuse definitions has been consistently upheld on policy grounds—specifically on the argument that it is important for authorities to retain flexibility to call injuries as they see them given that, particularly in a diverse society, abuse might appear in unexpected forms. The difficulty of the definitional project has also been acknowledged. This difficulty stems both from the relatively mundane problem of how textually to craft the definitions so that they capture all and only what we want them to capture, and from the related (but infinitely more complex) problem of how to resolve the ideological tensions at play in this area.

Each of these explanations has merit. First, we do not want to be left with definitions so fine that they disallow necessary protective interventions based in different (non-normative) or unprecedented and harmful parenting practices. Although such instances are infrequent, the CPS community's relatively recent experience with non-European immigrants who engage in unusual (for the United States) parenting practices, including family-formation practices, folk-medicine practices, and disciplinary practices, demonstrates that concerns about flexibility are both real and legitimate. Second, it is incredibly hard to craft precise statutory language; the annals of legislative history attest to the truth of this proposition. It is especially tricky to do so in an ethnically, religiously, and politically diverse setting like the United States, particularly when the context relates to the intersection of intimate family matters and the relationship of the state to the family. Legislators and elected judges operating in a legal context where definitions already exist are likely to be better off if they leave things alone; the alternative, at least politically, is unattractive: entering the culture war that inevitably would result from efforts to codify different rules that respectively privilege and de-privilege particular groups' parenting norms.

Three Negative Effects

Nonetheless, the premise of this [viewpoint] is that the distinction between permissible and impermissible corporal punishment is too important to leave to the only loosely guided discretion afforded by modern child abuse definitions. In particular, three negative effects of the status quo beg for at least a periodic reevaluation of the prospects for more precise tools to make this distinction. We have already noted two of these effects: the law's failure to fulfill its expressive function (or the law's signaling problems) and inconsistent case outcomes. The third is the risk of error in both directions—false-positive and false-negative findings of maltreatment—and the consequences of resulting errors for children and families. This risk is an inevitable result of the inconsistencies that plague the system. Importantly, errors (both ways) also occur because—other than those respecting egregious physical harm—the definitions do not codify a considered or generally accepted sense of the nature of the harm the state intends to prohibit. Again, this has been left mostly unresolved, either purposefully or by default. This means that the definitions fail to provide decision makers with information about the right kinds of cases to pursue. The ultimate objective of this [viewpoint] is to propose policy reforms that will ameliorate the risk of errors as well as the systemic inconsistencies and signaling problems already described.

Viable Policy Reforms

We proceed toward this end on the assumption that reforms will be viable in the long run only if they are the product of a careful accommodation of the delicate political considerations

The Difficulty of Drawing the Line

The defining aspect of corporal punishment, and indeed the key to its potential for securing short-term compliance, is that it involves inflicting pain on children. Even proponents of corporal punishment argue that it should be painful. As a country, Americans need to reevaluate why we believe it is reasonable to hit young, vulnerable children when it is against the law to hit other adults, prisoners, and even animals. The difficulty of drawing the line between physical abuse and corporal punishment begs the question Why should we risk harming our children when there are a range of alternative methods of punishment and discipline?

Elizabeth Thompson Gershoff, "Corporal Punishment, Physical Abuse, and the Burden of Proof: Reply to Baumrind, Larzelere, and Cowan (2002), Holden (2002), and Parke (2002)," Psychological Bulletin, *vol. 128, no. 4, 2002.*

at stake in matters of state—family relations and of the medical and social science evidence that explains when and how children suffer harm. Specifically, we suggest policy reforms that (1) preserve the traditional structure and substance of reasonable corporal punishment exceptions to child abuse law, both of which are themselves premised on a generous reading of parental-autonomy norms, and (2) require decision makers to take systematic and consistent account of all relevant and valid evidence, including medical and social science evidence, that can shed light on the reasonableness of parents' actions. We adopt this approach for two reasons.

First, it is the reality on the ground that parental-autonomy norms interact and even sometimes compete with medical and social science perspectives as the line is drawn in individual cases between reasonable corporal punishment and maltreatment. Although this [viewpoint] treats only the institutional actors, almost everyone involved in these cases uses one or the other or a hybrid approach to doing the line-drawing work required under the rules. This includes parents who use corporal punishment as a disciplinary tool; their neighbors who have to decide whether to report them for child abuse; CPS workers who process reports, investigate cases, and decide whether to substantiate them; and judges who adjudicate claims of excessive corporal punishment.

Second, although legal reform is sometimes warranted in the face of the status quo, we do not believe that such confrontation is necessary here. It makes sense that parental-autonomy norms and scientific knowledge should govern the process of arriving at better definitions of reasonable corporal punishment and physical abuse, and of sorting individual incidents and injuries along the continuum of non-accidental physical injuries. This approach best reflects what history and social science tells us is good for children: a child-rearing model that recognizes and establishes parents as the children's "first[,] best" caretakers and that intervenes in the family only when necessary to protect the child from harm that would be greater than that inevitably caused by the state's own intervention. This approach also reflects appropriate respect for parents' traditional role and the "rights and responsibilities" paradigm that has long governed American law in this area. Correspondingly, it acknowledges both that the state cannot replace parents as the children's "first[,] best" caretakers, and that the state has a proper role to play when parents make too much of their rights and too little of their responsibilities, causing a net loss to their children in the process.

A Standard of Functional Impairment

Given these considerations and our objectives—to ameliorate systemic inconsistencies, signaling problems, and false-positive and false-negative errors—our principal suggestion is for policy makers to codify "functional impairment" as the harm the state intends to prohibit. The term, adapted from the medical sciences, refers to short- or long-term or permanent impairment of emotional or physical functioning in tasks of daily living. (Currently, most states' maltreatment definitions prohibit practices and injuries that may lead to functional impairment.) Correspondingly, we encourage adoption of functional impairment as the standard for evaluating the reasonableness of the force used and thus for drawing the line between reasonable corporal punishment and abuse. We promote this standard to ensure that the state has the authority to intervene in the family in the face of good evidence that a child has suffered or risks suffering important disabilities, and to restrict state authority to intervene merely to mediate suboptimal conditions. Relatedly, this standard serves to assure, to the extent possible, that the public's wisdom regarding the normative use of corporal punishment is balanced with medical and scientific knowledge of harm to the child.

Basing decision making about the reasonableness of corporal punishment on a combination of parental-autonomy norms and scientific evidence about harm, as this functional-impairment test would do, is not new. For example, many maltreatment statutes and regulatory schemes are expressly premised on both a respect for family privacy and a focus on child well-being. And California's attorney general has suggested that scientific knowledge about the effectiveness of corporal punishment as a disciplinary tool should factor into the evaluation of whether it is legally reasonable to spank a toddler. However, these initiatives are not systematic and often lack rigor; they do not necessarily reflect a considered evaluation and reconciliation of the relevant norms and scientific knowledge, or of whether basing a decision on either or both in combination makes sense in a given situation. Nor have they ameliorated the negative effects that are our target: the failure of the law to fulfill its expressive function, inconsistent case analyses and outcomes, and false-positive and false-negative errors.

VIEWPOINT 

> *"Concluding that punishment, as a general method of discipline, does not work leads to other more disastrous fallout."*

Punishment Is Effective

Ennio Cipani

Ennio Cipani is a psychologist; a professor in the Department of Special Education at National University in Fresno, California; and the author of Punishment on Trial: A Resource Guide to Child Discipline. *In the following viewpoint excerpted from* Punishment on Trial, *he seeks to clear misunderstandings of punishing children and how punishment works. Cipani states that when a form of punishment does not stop misbehavior, two mistakes are made: parents believe that the child is resistant to punishment itself and discontinue discipline, or they increase the punishment's intensity or duration, which can lead to abuse. Rather, he insists, punishment only occurs when the offending behavior stops; punishment does not necessarily equate with the harshest consequences or spanking.*

As you read, consider the following questions:

1. What is the procedural definition of punishment, as provided by the author?

2. What does Cipani describe as a slippery slope?
3. According to the author, how can hugs be a punishment?

Punishment is not just a controversial topic, it is often misunderstood. It can mean apples to one group of people and bananas to another. Yet both groups would insist, in heated arguments, that they are talking about the same phenomenon. One group would describe apples, and their color, texture and shape. The other group would violently reject this supposition, saying that if one were not color-blind, one could plainly see that this phenomenon is yellow in color, and describe a banana. In other words, each group would describe a different phenomenon, but use the same term to define it.

How does the analogy about apples and bananas apply to punishment? Take a look at the examples below which are statements with a reference to punishment.

> "He really punished him by sending him to his room."

> "The boxer gave the challenger some punishing blows to the midsection."

> "The man's punishment for driving without a license was 6 months' probation."

> "The child was punished for grabbing the cereal off the shelf."

Which of the above are examples of punishment? It depends on your definition of punishment. There have certainly been numerous books and other writings on the topic of punishment. A cursory review of an online book distributor (www.barnesandnoble.com) found over 1,200 books listed under the subject heading of punishment. You would think that with all that material there would be agreement on the phenomenon described as punishment. The vast majority of these books deal with punishment from the judicial perspective. Punishment is often equated with the sentence a judge (or jury) hands down when a guilty verdict is given. It is the imposition of a harsh set of conditions, as a result of some offending behavior, which characterizes punishment in much of these writings.

The Procedural Definition of Punishment

This perspective of punishment exemplifies what I will term as the "procedural definition of punishment." This definition merely requires the existence of two temporally ordered events (referred to as a contingency). First, some law violation behavior occurs (perpetrator is caught and successfully prosecuted). Second, the consequence is the imposition of the sentence, which is deemed to be of an aversive nature to the individual.

The procedural definition best fits the common use of the term, punishment, when referring to examples of punishment. Punishment is viewed as the imposition of a harsh consequence for a child's misbehavior. There exists a conditional relationship between what the child does and a consequence that befalls him or her. If the child engages in misbehavior, then a harsh or aversive condition is imposed. This is how many people define punishment.

What are some examples of this procedural use of the term, punishment? If Johnny hits his sister, he will go to bed. If Suzie has a tantrum, she will be sent to the corner for 20 minutes. If Raul hits his mother, he will get spanked. According to the procedural definition, the existence of punishment is determined via a subjective judgment regarding the harshness of the consequence. Did Johnny, Suzy, and Raul all receive punishment? Well, that depends on you, the judge.

With regard to the first example, was punishment delivered to Johnny for hitting his sister? You might say "yes," but others may question whether being sent to bed for hitting one's sister really constitutes punishment. Their response might be along the following line: "Going to bed is a punishment for not eating your vegetables. It's not adequate for a child who hits his sister. You have to teach him a lesson. Something far worse should be done, like taking away TV time for a week. But only one night of punishment? This is not right."

As you can see, being sent to bed would not, in the eyes of some, constitute an appropriate consequence for hitting one's sister, particularly if the incident caused injury. Who is right? Just as beauty is in the eye of the beholder, so too is punishment when using a procedural definition. What is harsh to one person is mild to another.

A Common Mistake

Note that in the above examples, the effect on the child's behavior is not specified. I believe this to be a huge and common mistake in discussions of punishment and one that leads to the widespread misunderstanding of punishment. Why is it important to specify what the effect on behavior is? Let's use the third example above to illustrate the ambiguity one faces when using the procedural (but highly subjective) approach to defining punishment. When Raul hits his mother, he will get spanked. Raul engages in this undesirable behavior and the presumed harsh (aversive) consequence is applied, i.e., spanking. Let us imagine that this harsh consequence is not effective. In other words, Raul still hits his mother when he is mad at her for not letting him watch TV. What are we to conclude? Punishment does not work for Raul? As his mother might utter, "Raul is beyond that of normal mortals, he is unaffected by punishment." If a child is not fazed by punishment, what can possibly help? "Probably only some miracle behavior drug that has yet to be discovered," mutters Raul's mother.

The pitfall with the procedural definition is that it attempts to account for the success or failure of punishment on the basis of a given application. If some consequence, which appears to be so aversive that it should affect child behavior, does not work, punishment itself is determined to be ineffective.

Concluding that punishment, as a general method of discipline, does not work leads to other more disastrous fallout. When parents or adults conclude this, they often do one of two things. First, they may claim that punishment does not work for their particular child. If punishment does not work, what else can be done for their child? "No sense trying something else along the same lines," is the faulty reasoning here. The unfortunate by-product of this conclusion is giving up on the effort to change behavior via consequences. They justify this conclusion by explaining the existence of behavior in terms of an unalterable condition, a condition inherent in the child's biology. I have often heard the following as an explanation for the failure of a consequence to change behavior: "Well, you know Johnny is just Johnny. He does this because he is just being Johnny." Translation: Since punishment does not work, it is in Johnny's nature to do what he does and nothing is going to change that!

Alternatively, the adult may conclude that not enough punishment (meaning magnitude or amount) was administered. This can be potentially more dangerous in the hands of novices than simply giving up. Their solution is to alter the intensity or duration of the consequent event. If you were spanking him once for hitting you, maybe you should spank him twice, or thrice. Maybe you should pull his pants down so he will really feel it.

As you can readily see, this is a slippery slope. Many an abusive situation was unintentionally rendered in the search for a really, really harsh consequence, to effect a change in behavior. In the 1970s some children and adults living in institutions were sent to time-out: for two to three days in a box, with minimal food and water. The thought there must have been, if 2-hour time-outs were ineffective, maybe three days will do the trick. Failing to understand what constitutes punishment and how it works, I believe, is in large part, responsible for such abusive practices.

Punishment Is Outcome Oriented

Concluding nothing can work, or escalating consequences to unsafe levels, can be the downfall of a procedural definition. Such results are less likely when an "outcome-oriented definition" is used. In an outcome-oriented definition, a procedural contingency (i.e., temporal relationship between behavior and a consequence) is still existent. However, an additional requirement is that the effect of this contingency on the behavior is one of decrease. Punishment as a phenomenon exists when a procedural (behavioral) contingency produces a decrease in the level of the target behavior. If one is interested in decreasing a behavior, punishment always works!

With outcome-oriented punishment, there is no need to judge the harshness of the consequence. If Johnny gets sent to bed early when he hits his sister, and he stops hitting his sister as a function of that consequence, then punishment exists. One cannot judge the presence of punishment simply by examining the consequence. Rather one must know what behavioral effect resulted when such a contingency was put in place. This use of the term punishment leads to some interesting corollaries.

First, punishment does not necessarily equate with the most severe forms of consequences. Punishment can occur with a consequence that certainly does not evoke physical pain in the individual.... One need not be concerned about a subjective appraisal of the intended consequence. Rather one should be concerned with the resultant effect. This definition stipulates an outcome-oriented requirement.

Second, to equate the term punishment, with spankings, paddling, or any other form of corporal punishment is incorrect. In the previous example, if spanking produces a decrease in Raul hitting his mother, then punishment occurred. Spanking is a punisher in this situation. Spanking may not have the same effect with another child, or in another context. Further, one should not equate having a "tough" discipline practice with being effective. . . .

Punishment depends on the outcome of the contingency. If the procedural contingency produces a decrement in the behavior that is targeted, then punishment occurred. If it does not, then punishment did not occur, irrespective of the noxious nature of the consequence.

Perhaps this example can make the distinction even clearer. If I asked you, "Is having a teacher hug a student a reinforcer or a punisher," many of you would emphatically state it is a reinforcer. Forgive me for putting words in your mouth, but your rationale for such an evaluation is most likely that hugs are an inherent sign of care and affection, and therefore, should be considered a reinforcer. You probably can't see where getting a hug could be aversive, could you? But using the outcome-oriented definition, if a teacher hugs a child each time she says the correct answer to a problem and as a result the rate of correct answers decreases, we have punishment! I am sure you could now figure out some scenarios where hugging could result in the behavior it produces becoming less frequent. If you doubt this, start frequently hugging your teenager in front of his or her friends for some set of behaviors and watch those behaviors disappear from their repertoire! Now there is a discipline strategy I bet you never thought of before reading this [viewpoint]! . . .

Punishing Behavior, Not the Person

The outcome-oriented definition of punishment also leads to an important distinction. As a behavior analyst, I view punishment as something that occurs to a behavior. Contrast this with the common conception of punishment, i.e., you punish the person. This is a significant distinction. When I use punishment, I desire to decrease a behavior by producing an effective behavioral contingency that alters that behavior. What is the objective when you punish a person? What behavior or behaviors do you intend to alter? Or is altering a behavior a concern at all? As a side note, the same mistake is often heard in reference to reinforcement (i.e., reinforce a person). If you hear someone claim they reinforce the child, tell them that people cannot get reinforced. How does one increase a person? Rather, a behavior is reinforced (i.e., strengthened in future probability).

VIEWPOINT

"Surprisingly, the most effective discipline typically doesn't involve any punishment at all, but instead focuses on positive reinforcement when children are being good."

Positive Reinforcement Is More Effective than Punishment

Tara Parker-Pope

In the following viewpoint, Tara Parker-Pope proposes that commonly used punishments reinforce the misbehaviors parents attempt to correct. Instead, she states, the most effective discipline for children and adolescents is positive reinforcement. A study revealed that a third of parents who used time-outs, revoking privileges, yelling, and spanking failed to discipline their children, says Parker-Pope, because children learn that being bad attracts more attention than being good. Therefore, the author recommends that parents pay attention to and spend time with children when they are behaving. A health writer for the New York Times, *Parker-Pope contributes to its* Well *blog and has authored numerous health books.*

Tara Parker-Pope, "It's Not Discipline, It's a Teachable Moment," *New York Times*, September 15, 2008.

As you read, consider the following questions:

1. As stated in the viewpoint, why is effective discipline difficult for busy parents?
2. When are time-outs as punishments rendered ineffective, as suggested by Parker-Pope?
3. As described by Parker-Pope, what are the best methods of keeping adolescents out of trouble?

Whether facing a toddler temper tantrum or an insolent adolescent, every parent struggles to find the best way to discipline children.

But many parents fail. A recent study found that 1 in 3 say the methods they use simply don't work.

The problem may not be the kids so much as the way parents define discipline. Childhood health experts say many parents think discipline means meting out punishment. But often the punishments parents use end up reinforcing the bad behavior instead of correcting it. Surprisingly, the most effective discipline typically doesn't involve any punishment at all, but instead focuses on positive reinforcement when children are being good.

Dr. Kenneth Ginsburg, adolescent medicine specialist at Children's Hospital of Philadelphia, said that when parents come to him complaining of discipline problems, he often explains the etymology of the word. The Latin root is "discipulus," which means student or pupil.

"Defining discipline is really important," said Dr. Ginsburg, author of *A Parent's Guide to Building Resilience in Children and Teens*, published by the American Academy of Pediatrics. "When I tell parents this, you see their faces and they say: 'It's not about punishment? It's about teaching?' That changes things."

But effective discipline is more difficult for busy parents because strategies that involve teaching and positive feedback take a lot more time than simple punishment, noted Dr. Shari Barkin, chief of the division of general pediatrics at the Monroe Carell Jr. Children's Hospital at Vanderbilt University.

It was Dr. Barkin's study of more than 2,100 parents that reported that 1 in 3 said they could not effectively discipline their kids. The findings, published last year [2007] in the journal *Clinical Pediatrics*, showed that parents often used the same punishments that their own parents had used on them. Forty-five percent reported using time-outs, 41.5 percent said they removed privileges, 13 percent reported yelling at their children and 8.5 percent said they used spanking "often or always."

Parents who resorted to yelling or spanking were far more likely to say their disciplinary approach was ineffective. Given that parents often don't admit to yelling and spanking, the study probably underestimates how widespread the problem of ineffective discipline really is, Dr. Barkin said.

Capturing Parents' Attention

Many parents' discipline methods don't work because children quickly learn that it's much easier to capture a parent's attention with bad behavior than with good. Parents unwittingly reinforce this by getting on the phone, sending e-mail messages or reading the paper as soon as a child starts playing quietly, and by stopping the activity and scolding a child when he starts to misbehave.

"How many times have you heard someone say, 'I need to get off the phone because my child is acting up'?" asked Dr. Nathan J. Blum, a developmental-behavioral pediatrician at Children's Hospital of Philadelphia. "You're doing exactly what the child wants."

Trying to reason with a child who is misbehaving doesn't work. "Talking and lecturing and even yelling is essentially giving kids your attention," Dr. Blum said.

Reinforcement vs. Reward

Most people use the words *reward* and *reinforcer* interchangeably. In many cases rewards do function as reinforcers. However, the words *reinforcement* and *reinforcer* have functional meaning that is not explicit in the term *reward.* A reward is something given for special behavior. But, a reward is not necessarily a consequence of a behavior, is usually not given repeatedly, and most importantly does not have the explicit meaning of an increased rate of the behavior that the reward was given for. In contrast, a *reinforcer is a contingent,* explicit *consequence* of a behavior, usually occurring repeatedly, which *by definition increases the rate of the preceding behavior.* . . . If a behavior is "rewarded," but the rate of the behavior does not increase, then the behavior was not reinforced and reinforcement did not occur. Rewarding a behavior with a gold star will not necessarily reinforce (i.e., select or increase the rate of) the behavior that was rewarded.

Stephen Ray Flora, The Power of Reinforcement. *Albany: State University of New York Press, 2004.*

While time-outs can be highly effective for helping young children calm down and regain control of their emotions, many parents misuse the technique, doctors say. Parents often lecture or scold children during time-outs or battle with kids to return to a time-out chair. But giving a child any attention during a time-out will render the technique ineffective.

Another problem is that parents miscalculate how long a time-out should last. A child in an extended time-out will become bored and start to misbehave again to win attention. Doctors advise no more than a minute of time-out for each year of a child's life.

A better disciplinary method for younger children doesn't focus on bad behavior but on good behavior, Dr. Blum said. If children are behaving well, get off the phone or stop what you are doing and make a point to tell them that you wanted to spend time with them because they are so well behaved.

Discipline in the Teenage Years

Discipline is more difficult in the teenage years as children struggle to gain independence. Studies show that punishments like grounding have little effect on teenagers' behavior. In several studies of youth drinking, drug use and early sex, the best predictor for good behavior wasn't punishment, but parental monitoring and involvement. The best methods of keeping teenagers out of trouble are knowing where they are, knowing who is with them, and spending time with them regularly.

That doesn't mean teenagers shouldn't be punished. But parents should set clear rules that allow children to earn or lose privileges, which gives them a sense that they control their destiny.

"You don't want kids to feel victimized or punished," said Dr. Ginsburg of Children's Hospital of Philadelphia. "You want them to understand that the freedoms they get are directly related to how they demonstrate responsibility."

Dr. Barkin said she believed the problem of ineffective discipline was getting worse, in part because reinforcing good behavior is far more time-consuming than punishment. Dr. Barkin noted that busy parents juggling work and family demands often are distracted by cell phones, e-mail and other media.

"We have these new forms of technology which urge us to be working all the time," Dr. Barkin said. "We are a distracted society. It's harder to turn off the media and turn on that personal engagement."

VIEWPOINT 

"Lately the art of family discipline has begun to reflect our digital age."

Grounding Teens from Using Technology Can Be Effective

Donna St. George

Donna St. George is a staff writer for the Washington Post. *In the following viewpoint, she states that as social media and mobile technology become central to the lives of children and adolescents, parents are resorting to "digital" grounding as a means of discipline. For instance, St. George cites a 2010 poll indicating that 62 percent of parents took away cell phones as a form of punishment. Privileges to use Facebook, handheld devices, and video games are increasingly revoked from children, she explains. For digital grounding to be most effective, experts recommend that the consequences should be related to the wrongdoing, says St. George.*

As you read, consider the following questions:

1. How has technology changed growing up for teenagers, as stated by St. George?

Donna St. George, "Parents Use 'Digital' Grounding as a 21st Century Disciplinary Tool," *Washington Post*, September 5, 2010.

2. How does Richard Weissbourd describe the threat of losing digital privileges?
3. According to St. George, in what situations does taking a cell phone make sense and not make sense?

Not so long ago, teenagers in trouble got grounded. They lost their evenings out, maybe the keys to the family car. But lately the art of family discipline has begun to reflect our digital age.

Now parents seize cell phones, shut down Facebook pages, pull the plug on PlayStation.

That's how it went in Silver Spring [Maryland] last school year, when Iantha Carley's high schooler got a midterm grade report that contained letters of the alphabet that were not A, B or C.

Carley decreed there would be no more Facebook until he delivered a report card with better grades. The result: six weeks off-line. "He lived," Carley reports, "with no lasting damage."

Her approach has become increasingly common as technology has changed so much about growing up, including what teenagers value most. For the digital generation, the priority isn't always going out with friends. It's being with them—in text, online.

As another school year begins, and parents hold their children accountable for what happens in and out of the classroom, the threat of losing digital privileges will be a recurring flashpoint.

"It's a modern version of grounding," says Richard Weissbourd, a Harvard psychologist and author of *The Parents We Mean to Be*. "It's like taking away a weekend or a couple of weekends. It's a deprivation of social connections in the same way."

In a report earlier this year [2010] that captured part of the trend, 62 percent of parents said they had taken away a cell phone as punishment, according to the Pew Internet & American Life Project.

Parents "know how important and vital it is to their teens' existence," says the report's co-author Amanda Lenhart. "They were getting them where it hurt."

In Silver Spring, Carley, 53, is a believer in technology's power.

A week before her son, Ian Winick, came home with slipping grades, Carley had restricted his cell phone privileges because he over-texted for a second month.

Seeing the grades made her conclude: "He can't handle all of this. He just really needs to be unplugged."

They talked, and her view was: "You're not entitled to Facebook, you're not entitled to a cell phone. You need to find a way to make these things fit into your life—not become your life."

Carley changed her son's Facebook password, so he could not sign on to the site for his period of banishment.

Suddenly Ian, then a sophomore at Northwood High School, found himself out of the social loop. He began using e-mail more than he ever had. "I had to call people on the phone and stuff, which was weird because I wasn't used to doing it," he says.

Worse, the ban extended over last winter break, when social connections were even more important because school was out.

His mother did not relent. "I'm hard-core," she says.

Only after the teen's report card arrived, showing a 3.25 average for the quarter, did Carley return her son's cell phone and restore his Facebook privileges. "It was amazing how much better he did in school because he didn't have the distraction," she says.

Ian, now 16, acknowledges as much.

"I definitely did a lot better when that stuff was taken away," he says.

Now, he is more moderate in his Facebook and texting habits. "I don't want to have it happen to me again," he says.

Still, Carley says, her choice of discipline led to a few raised eyebrows among other parents. "Really?" she recalls being asked. "I said, 'It's not as hard as you think.'"

She amends: "Well, maybe for the first couple of days."

Expanding the Toolbox

The way Chelsea Welsh, 17, sees the phenomenon, parents have not necessarily switched tactics for her generation, so much as expanded them.

"We still get grounded," said Welsh, who goes to Oakcrest School in McLean [Virginia], "but grounded now includes cell phones and Facebook being taken away.

"It's an umbrella term," she says.

Experts point out that the word discipline actually means to teach and suggest it should be approached that way.

Some go further, saying consequences should be related to the transgression: that taking away a cell phone makes sense for breaking rules about texting, but perhaps not for coming home late; in that case, the consequence might include curfew times.

"The easiest thing to do is take away what your child values in hopes they'll correct their behavior to get it back, but that's going to feel like punishment, not like discipline," says Kenneth R. Ginsburg, author of *A Parent's Guide to Building Resilience in Children and Teens*, published by the American Academy of Pediatrics.

Still, parents say the threat of restrictions on Facebook or texting are persuasive as little else.

In University Park [Maryland], Michele Leonardi, 48, a mother of four, scaled back Facebook privileges after one of her 14-year-old twins had a "lapse in good judgment" several weeks ago while his friends were over. She doesn't want to say what went wrong, but says she required him to "friend" her on Facebook, so she could monitor his wall.

Her view is that "they deserve privacy as long as they don't violate my trust." But the teen's mistake set him back—not forever, she said, but "until I feel comfortable again."

In Alexandria [Virginia], Sarah Wholey, 42, recalls that when her 15-year-old son forgot to lock the family's townhouse—in spite of many lapses and reminders—his Xbox disappeared for a week. It was not because the family had a break-in. "It really did work," Wholey said. "He locked the house, and he didn't lose so many keys."

When the teen was disrespectful another day, he lost his cell phone. "He got angry at first, but then he came around, and said, 'You're right. I was being rude,'" his mother recalls.

Carrot and Stick

Cheryl Juneau, 44, mom of two sons in Alexandria, is well acquainted with the idea of technology as a motivator. Several months ago, her 10- and 12-year-old sons got iPod Touch devices, on which they love to play such games as JellyCar 2 and Angry Birds.

But the boys, who get an hour of screen time a day, can't play with their iPods before beds are made and the playroom is clean. Never before has Juneau seen her sons approach these chores with such determination, she says.

One recent August day, she used the technology a little differently.

One son had a mishap involving a squirt gun and an ill-advised shove. The conflict that followed did not go well.

"I just said, 'That's it. You do not get to use your iPod Touch tomorrow.'"

For her son, she says, it was "an aha moment." She says it started a conversation about what happened, why the privilege was withdrawn, what it felt like to be the other person in the scuffle, and who her son really wanted to be.

It was a compelling message, she says. "I can't think of anything else I could take away that would be more keenly felt."

VIEWPOINT

> *"Could it be that by protecting our kids from unhappiness as children, we're depriving them of happiness as adults?"*

Parents Should Allow Children to Experience Unhappiness and Pain

Lori Gottlieb

In the following viewpoint, Lori Gottlieb warns that parents who always protect their children from negative feelings—unhappiness, pain, and disappointment—can undermine their children's self-esteem and how they cope with challenges and hardships. Exposure to discomfort, failure, and struggle can help kids develop "psychological immunity," she reports. By not allowing children to experience sadness or anxiety, parents send the message that children cannot handle or accept these emotions, difficult events, and unhappiness as a normal part of life, the author maintains. Based in Beverly Hills, California, Gottlieb is a writer, therapist, consultant, and contributing editor to the Atlantic.

As you read, consider the following questions:

1. In what ways has the pursuit of happiness changed in America, in the author's view?

Lori Gottlieb, "How to Land Your Children in Therapy," *Atlantic*, July/August 2011.

2. How does the author use the example of a toddler falling in a park to demonstrate helping a child to feel secure?
3. How does the author react to parenting that obsesses with children's success at the expense of their happiness?

Child rearing has long been a touchy subject in America, perhaps because the stakes are so high and the theories so inconclusive. In her book *Raising America: Experts, Parents, and a Century of Advice About Children*, Ann Hulbert recounts how there's always been a tension among the various recommended parenting styles—the bonders versus the disciplinarians, the child centered versus the parent centered—with the pendulum swinging back and forth between them over the decades. Yet the underlying goal of good parenting, even during the heyday of don't-hug-your-kid-too-much advice in the 1920s ("When you are tempted to pet your child, remember that mother love is a dangerous instrument," the behavioral psychologist John Watson wrote in his famous guide to child rearing), has long been the same: to raise children who will grow into productive, happy adults. My parents certainly wanted me to be happy, and my grandparents wanted my parents to be happy too. What seems to have changed in recent years, though, is the way we think about and define happiness, both for our children and for ourselves.

Focusing Obsessively on Happiness

Nowadays, it's not enough to be happy—if you can be even happier. The American Dream and the pursuit of happiness have morphed from a quest for general contentment to the idea that you must be happy at all times and in every way. "I *am* happy," writes Gretchen Rubin in *The Happiness Project*, a book that topped the *New York Times* best-seller list and that has spawned something of a national movement in happiness seeking, "but I'm not as happy as I should be."

How happy *should* she be? Rubin isn't sure. She sounds exactly like some of my patients. She has two wonderful parents; a "tall, dark, and handsome" (and wealthy) husband she loves; two healthy, "delightful" children; a strong network of friends; a beautiful neo-Georgian mansion on the Upper East Side; a law degree from Yale; and a successful career as a freelance writer. Still, Rubin writes, she feels "dissatisfied, that something [is] missing." So to counteract her "bouts of melancholy, insecurity, listlessness, and free-floating guilt," she goes on a "happiness journey," making lists and action items, buying three new magazines every Monday for a month, and obsessively organizing her closets.

At one point during her journey, Rubin admits that she still struggles, despite the charts and resolutions and yearlong effort put into being happy. "In some ways," she writes, "I'd made myself less happy." Then she adds, citing one of her so-called Secrets of Adulthood, "Happiness doesn't always make you feel happy."

Modern social science backs her up on this. "Happiness as a by-product of living your life is a great thing," Barry Schwartz, a professor of social theory at Swarthmore College, told me. "But happiness as a goal is a recipe for disaster." It's precisely this goal, though, that many modern parents focus on obsessively—only to see it backfire. Observing this phenomenon, my colleagues and I began to wonder: Could it be that by protecting our kids from unhappiness as children, we're depriving them of happiness as adults?

"Psychological Immunity"

Paul Bohn, a psychiatrist at UCLA [the University of California, Los Angeles] who came to speak at my clinic, says the answer may be yes. Based on what he sees in his practice, Bohn believes many parents will do anything to avoid having their kids experience even mild discomfort, anxiety, or disappointment—"anything less than pleasant," as he puts it—with the result that when, as adults, they experience the normal frustrations of life, they think something must be terribly wrong.

Consider a toddler who's running in the park and trips on a rock, Bohn says. Some parents swoop in immediately, pick up the toddler, and comfort her in that moment of shock, before she even starts crying. But, Bohn explains, this actually prevents her from feeling secure—not just on the playground, but in life. If you don't let her experience that momentary confusion, give her the space to figure out what just happened (*Oh, I tripped*), and then briefly let her grapple with the frustration of having fallen and perhaps even try to pick herself up, she has no idea what discomfort feels like, and will have no framework for how to recover when she feels discomfort later in life. These toddlers become the college kids who text their parents with an SOS if the slightest thing goes wrong, instead of attempting to figure out how to deal with it themselves. If, on the other hand, the child trips on the rock, and the parents let her try to reorient for a second *before* going over to comfort her, the child learns: *That was scary for a second, but I'm okay now. If something unpleasant happens, I can get through it.* In many cases, Bohn says, the child recovers fine on her own—but parents never learn this, because they're too busy protecting their kid when she doesn't need protection.

Which made me think, of course, of my own sprints across the sand the second my toddler would fall. And of the time when he was 4 and a friend of mine died of cancer and I considered . . . not telling him! After all, he didn't even know she'd been sick (once, commenting on her head scarves, he'd asked me if she was an Orthodox Jew, and like a wuss, I said no, she just really likes scarves). I knew he might notice that we didn't see her anymore, but all of the parenting LISTSERVs I consulted said that hearing about a parent's death would be too scary for a child, and that, without lying (because God forbid that we enlightened, attuned parents ever lie to our children), I should sugarcoat it in all these ways that I knew would never withstand my preschooler's onslaught of cross-examining *whys*.

In the end, I told my son the truth. He asked a lot of questions, but he did not faint from the shock. If anything, according to Bohn, my trusting him to handle the news probably made him more trusting of me, and ultimately more emotionally secure. By telling him, I was communicating that I believed he could tolerate sadness and anxiety, and that I was here to help him through it. Not telling him would have sent a very different message: that I didn't feel he could handle discomfort. And that's a message many of us send our kids in subtle ways every day.

Dan Kindlon, a child psychologist and lecturer at Harvard, warns against what he calls our "discomfort with discomfort" in his book *Too Much of a Good Thing: Raising Children of Character in an Indulgent Age*. If kids can't experience painful feelings, Kindlon told me when I called him not long ago, they won't develop "psychological immunity."

"It's like the way our body's immune system develops," he explained. "You have to be exposed to pathogens, or your body won't know how to respond to an attack. Kids also need exposure to discomfort, failure, and struggle. I know parents who call up the school to complain if their kid doesn't get to be in the school play or make the cut for the baseball team. I know of one kid who said that he didn't like another kid in the carpool, so instead of having their child learn to tolerate the other kid, they offered to drive him to school themselves. By the time they're teenagers, they have no experience with hardship. Civilization is about adapting to less-than-perfect situations, yet parents often have this instantaneous reaction to unpleasantness, which is 'I can fix this.'"

Wendy Mogel is a clinical psychologist in Los Angeles who, after the publication of her book *The Blessing of a Skinned Knee* a decade ago, became an adviser to schools all

Letting Go Is Part of Love

An overprotective parent can be just as harmful as a parent who gives no protection. Good parents recognize the need to let their children go out on their own. Good parents guide and suggest and sometimes intervene, but as a whole, there comes a time when children have to be released, even if releasing them may cause them harm and pain. Good parents have to let go. Letting go is part of love. *Control is not love.*

Max Davis, It's Only a Flat Tire in the Rain: Navigating Life's Bumpy Roads with Faith and Grace. *New York: G.P. Putnam's Sons, 2001.*

over the country. When I talked to her this spring, she said that over the past few years, college deans have reported receiving growing numbers of incoming freshmen they've dubbed "teacups" because they're so fragile that they break down anytime things don't go their way. "Well-intentioned parents have been metabolizing their anxiety for them their entire childhoods," Mogel said of these kids, "so they don't know how to deal with it when they grow up."

Confusing Parents' Needs with Children's Needs

Which might be how people . . . end up in therapy. "You can have the best parenting in the world and you'll still go through periods where you're not happy," Jeff Blume, a family psychologist with a busy practice in Los Angeles, told me when I spoke to him recently. "A kid needs to feel normal anxiety to be resilient. If we want our kids to grow up and be more independent, then we should prepare our kids to leave us every day."

But that's a big if. Blume believes that many of us today don't really want our kids to leave, because we rely on them in various ways to fill the emotional holes in our own lives. Kindlon and Mogel both told me the same thing. Yes, we devote inordinate amounts of time, energy, and resources to our children, but for whose benefit?

"We're confusing our own needs with our kids' needs and calling it good parenting," Blume said, letting out a sigh. I asked him why he sighed. (This is what happens when two therapists have a conversation.) "It's sad to watch," he explained. "I can't tell you how often I have to say to parents that they're putting too much emphasis on their kids' feelings because of their own issues. If a *therapist* is telling you to pay *less* attention to your kid's feelings, you know something has gotten way of out of whack." . . .

"Would you rather make your kid mad at you by arguing over cleaning up his room, or play a game of Boggle together? We don't set limits, because we want our kids to like us at every moment, even though it's better for them if sometimes they can't stand us."

Kindlon also observed that because we tend to have fewer kids than past generations of parents did, each becomes more precious. So we demand more from them—more companionship, more achievement, more happiness. Which is where the line between selflessness (making our kids happy) and selfishness (making ourselves happy) becomes especially thin.

"We want our kids to be happy living the life we envision for them—the banker who's happy, the surgeon who's happy," Barry Schwartz, the Swarthmore social scientist, told me, even though those professions "might not actually make them happy." At least for parents of a certain demographic (and if you're reading this [viewpoint], you're likely among them), "we're not so happy if our kids work at Walmart but show up each day with a smile on their faces," Schwartz says. "They're happy, but we're not. Even though we say what we want most for our kids is their happiness, and we'll do everything we can to help them achieve that, it's unclear where parental happiness ends and our children's happiness begins."

His comment reminded me of a conversation I'd just had with a camp director when I inquired about the program. She was going down the list of activities for my child's age group, and when she got to basketball, T-ball, and soccer, she quickly added, "But of course, it's all noncompetitive. We don't encourage competition." I had to laugh: all of these kids being shunted away from "competition" as if it were kryptonite. Not to get too shrink-y, but could this be a way for parents to work out their ambivalence about their own competitive natures?

Parental Overinvestment and Generational Narcissism

It may be this question—and our unconscious struggle with it—that accounts for the scathing reaction to Amy Chua's memoir, *Battle Hymn of the Tiger Mother*, earlier this year [in 2011]. Chua's efforts "not to raise a soft, entitled child" were widely attacked on blogs and mommy LISTSERVs as abusive, yet that didn't stop the book from spending several months on the *New York Times* best-seller list. Sure, some parents might have read it out of pure voyeurism, but more likely, Chua's book resonated so powerfully because she isn't so different from her critics. She may have been obsessed with her kids' success at the expense of their happiness—but many of today's parents who are obsessed with their kids' happiness share Chua's drive, just wrapped in a prettier package. Ours is a have-your-cake-and-eat-it-too approach, a desire for high achievement without the sacrifice and struggle that this kind of achievement often requires. When the Tiger Mom looked unsparingly at her parental contradictions, perhaps she made the rest of us squirm because we were forced to examine our own.

Chua, says Wendy Mogel, "was admitting in such a candid way what loads of people think but just don't own up to." In her practice, Mogel meets many parents who let kids off the hook for even basic, simple chores so they can spend more time on homework. Are these parents being too lenient (letting the chores slide), or too hard-core (teaching that good grades are more important than being a responsible family member)? Mogel and Dan Kindlon agree that whatever form it takes—whether the fixation is happiness or success—parental overinvestment is contributing to a burgeoning generational narcissism that's hurting our kids.

Periodical and Internet Sources Bibliography

The following articles have been selected to supplement the diverse views presented in this chapter.

James H. Burnett	"What if Spanking Works?," *Boston Globe Magazine*, June 17, 2012.
Ira J. Chasnoff	"Catch 'Em Being Good," *Aristotle's Child* (blog), *Psychology Today*, May 27, 2011.
Megan Clarke	"Nobody Deserves a Good Spanking," *U.S. Catholic*, June 2008.
Kathy Custren	"Grounding and Time-Out," *OM Times Magazine*, November 10, 2011.
Pamela Druckerman	"Why French Parents Are Superior," *Wall Street Journal*, February 4, 2012.
Katia Hetter	"Punishment Without Spanking," CNN.com, November 8, 2011.
NPR	"'E-Grounding' Parents' New Disciplinary Weapon," December 8, 2010. www.npr.org.
Bonnie Rochman	"The First Real-Time Study of Parents Spanking Their Kids," *Time*, June 28, 2011.
Darshak Sanghavi	"Spank No More," *Slate*, December 13, 2011.
Brendan L. Smith	"The Case Against Spanking," *APA Monitor on Psychology*, April 2012.
Hilary Stout	"For Some Parents, Shouting Is the New Spanking," *New York Times*, October 21, 2009.

CHAPTER 2

Do Some Forms of Parenting Put Children at a Disadvantage?

Chapter Preface

Transracial parenting is a common adoption arrangement in the United States. For instance, 40 percent of children in international adoptions have a different racial or cultural background than their parents, according to the US Department of Health and Human Services in a 2007 survey. "The issue is getting more media attention as white stars in Hollywood—including Sandra Bullock, Tom Cruise, Hugh Jackman, Michelle Pfeiffer, Madonna, and Charlize Theron—adopt children from other racial groups," observes Rose Russell, a staff writer for the *Toledo Blade.*

For many years, adoption agencies reportedly encouraged parents to take a color-blind approach in transracial parenting. "Social workers used to tell parents, 'You just raise your child as though you gave birth to her,'" says Adam Pertman, executive director of the Evan B. Donaldson Adoption Institute, in an interview with National Public Radio (NPR). "An extreme majority of transracially adopted kids . . . grew up wishing they were white or thinking they were white, not wanting to look in mirrors," explains Pertman. David Watts, a biracial social worker, believes that being raised by white parents prevented him from fully realizing his identity as a black man. "I didn't realize the difference between white and black culture until I was 21 and came to New York. That's when I learned what I had missed, not only the obvious things, like food and dress and music, but the subtleties of black culture—the jokes told, how loud you speak, how much you touch when you talk, the relationships between mothers and sons," he says. "That's when I realized that while my parents had done a good job, it was incomplete, because I didn't have the full story."

Nonetheless, some research reports that transracial parenting does not have a negative impact on kids. In a longitudinal twenty-year study of black and Korean adoptees in more than two hundred families, 80 percent of respondents said that racial differences were not crucial, stressing the importance of loving and secure family relationships. "You can love the adopted child as if he or she was your own, but if you're adopting across racial lines, you have to make changes. You cannot raise a child as if that child was a white child. Some parents learned that faster than others," declares Rita Simon, a public affairs professor at American University, who conducted the study. In the following chapter, the authors deliberate whether some types of parenting place children at a disadvantage.

Viewpoint 

> *"Parenting a child is a two-person job best performed by a husband and wife."*

Young Unmarried Women and Men Should Not Be Parents

Deborrah Cooper

Deborrah Cooper is a dating expert and advice columnist based in Northern California. She conducts workshops as well as produces and hosts Date Smarter, Not Harder, *an online radio talk show. In the following viewpoint, Cooper argues that unmarried women and men are unprepared to face parenthood alone and that single parenting endangers the well-being and lives of children. She persists that kids in single-parent homes suffer much higher rates of abuse, neglect, serious injury, and maltreatment than those in two-parent families. Consequently, Cooper urges women to recognize the realities of parenting and choose pregnancy only after marriage and reaching their educational and professional goals.*

As you read, consider the following questions:

1. What figures does Cooper cite for the higher risk of physical and emotional abuse and neglect for children of single parents?

Deborrah Cooper, "When the Children of Single Parents End Up Dead," *Surviving Dating*, September 21, 2011.

2. As described by Cooper, what factors contribute to the higher rates of abuse among young parents?
3. Why do many young women fantasize about having a baby, in Cooper's view?

In June 2011, a 20-year-old single mother living in Chicago beat and suffocated her 3-month-old son because he wouldn't stop crying. The next morning she strapped him into a Baby Bjorn and went shopping with the dead infant as if nothing were wrong.

A 21-year-old New York mom smacked her 5-year-old son so hard in his stomach and back that he died five days later of internal injuries. She was furious because he broke the television while playing Nintendo Wii.

In Jacksonville, Florida, a 22-year-old mom was arrested for shaking her three-month-old son to death. She is reported to have told police that she shook the baby, smoked a cigarette "to compose herself," and then shook him again. She was upset because his crying interrupted her playing an online video game.

A Knotts Island, North Carolina, 16-year-old teenager went to a hospital emergency room to report that she had given birth to a baby and the baby died. Police came to her home and turned it [the baby] over to the medical examiner for autopsy. Findings: the newborn died of multiple stab wounds inflicted by its teenaged mother.

A 31-year-old Ohio woman was recently convicted of killing her 28-day-old baby girl. She placed her daughter in a microwave oven and turned it on, reportedly distraught after a fight with her boyfriend over whether or not he was the baby's biological father.

Finally, just last week [in September 2011] a 25-year-old St. Louis mother of three was charged with two counts of first-degree murder. She is accused of killing her 5-year-old son and 4-year-old daughter with a shotgun by shooting them in the head. Her oldest child, an 8-year-old boy, was able to escape the carnage. Her relatives are defending her by claiming she is bipolar and on antidepressant medication. Isn't it interesting though that not one of them thought it might be important to protect the children by removing them from the care of their mentally ill mother?

Young fathers are not immune to the pressure of parenting themselves.

A 22-year-old New Orleans father confessed murdering his toddler son to avoid paying $4,000 in back child support. After his story that the child was abducted was disproven, he admitted to stuffing the child's body in a bag and dumping it in a playground.

A young father who by all accounts was nothing but "a normal guy" living with his girlfriend and new baby was arrested and charged with murdering his four-month-old. The baby was found to be suffering from brain bleeds, skull fractures, and multiple rib fractures.

In Houston, an allegedly mature 31-year-old father admitted to punching his 5-month-old daughter in the abdomen so hard he killed her. He was angry because she wouldn't stop crying.

In Los Angeles, a 17-year-old father kidnapped his 5-month-old baby after calling the child's mother and threatening to hurt the child. An Amber Alert was issued. When police saw the suspect and attempted to stop him, he fatally stabbed the infant. Deputies, helpless to stop him, watched in horror.

What is it about parenting that causes young men and women to be neglectful, abusive, and to react with violence toward infants and toddlers?

Child Abuse: What Is It, and Who Is Most Affected?

Each state has laws which define abusive acts which may be addressed in criminal or civil courts. However, the U.S. Child

Abuse Prevention and Treatment Act (CAPTA) defines child abuse and neglect as:

> Any recent act or failure to act on the part of a parent or caretaker, which results in death, serious physical or emotional harm, sexual abuse, or exploitation, or an act or failure to act which presents an imminent risk of serious harm.

CAPTA goes on to provide a detailed explanation of sexual abuse, which includes:

> The employment, use, persuasion, inducement, enticement, or coercion of any child to engage in, or assist any other person to engage in, any sexually explicit conduct or simulation of such conduct for the purpose of producing a visual depiction of such conduct; or
>
> The rape, and in cases of caretaker or interfamilial relationships, statutory rape, molestation, prostitution, or other form of sexual exploitation of children, or incest with children.

According to statistics, young children are the most vulnerable; one-third of the reported victims of child abuse were under the age of four. More children 0–4 years of age in the United States die from homicide than from infectious diseases or cancer. In the United States, an average of four children die every single day due to abuse and neglect.

Young children at the highest risk of homicide are those under age one. Homicides of children in this group include a certain number of infanticides (homicides in which recently born children are killed by relatives who do not want the child, are ill-equipped to care for the child, or are suffering from a childbirth-related psychiatric disturbance).

Children living in single-parent homes also experienced:

- 77 percent greater risk of being physically abused

- 87 percent greater risk of being harmed by physical neglect
- 165 percent greater risk of experiencing notable physical neglect
- 74 percent greater risk of suffering from emotional neglect
- 80 percent greater risk of suffering serious injury as a result of abuse
- 120 percent greater risk of experiencing some type of maltreatment overall.

The age of the child's mother has also been shown to influence the child's risks for mistreatment. Younger mothers have statistically higher rates of child abuse than mature moms. Lack of economic resources, the stress of single parenting, social isolation, and a dearth of emotional support are factors which contribute to the higher rate of abuse among young parents.

The Reality of Parenting

Many young women get caught up in the fantasy of pregnancy as the cure-all for loneliness, a lack of family, or a lack of love. Some believe that having a child "for him" will be the ultimate gift . . . the glue that will hold a male's attention and keep him involved in a relationship forever. Other young women believe that since they were raised in a single-parent home and turned out "okay" that they can and should do the same.

Focusing on the "miracle of life" and "the blessing" they have been told they are carrying, many young women begin shopping for baby clothes and accessories. Their days are spent fantasizing about life as a proud mother of a beautiful little baby girl or boy. Amazingly, there is little to no focus on

The Economic Toll of Single Parenthood

The poverty rate for single moms and dads is much higher than for married couples. The chart shows families with children under 18 whose incomes fall below the poverty level.

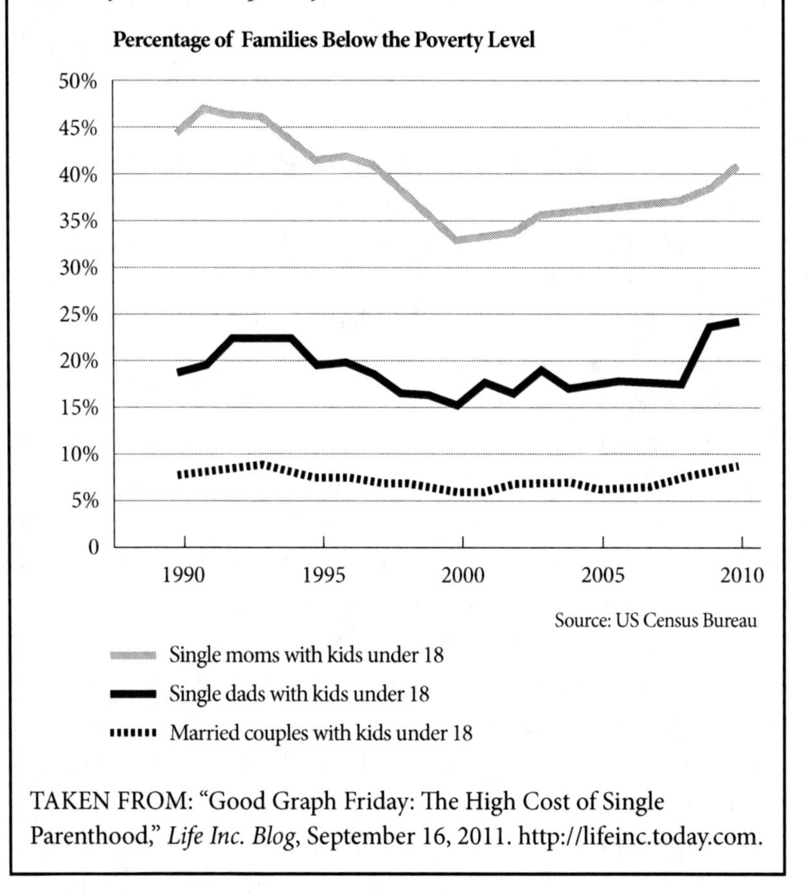

TAKEN FROM: "Good Graph Friday: The High Cost of Single Parenthood," *Life Inc. Blog*, September 16, 2011. http://lifeinc.today.com.

how drastically different life will be once they are saddled down with the burdensome responsibility of raising a child on their own.

It is not until the child is born that the reality of parenting hits. You will see then how exhausted you are, how broke you are, how people get tired of hearing your child cry so they refuse to babysit. You will see how your baby's father goes on about his business having fun with his friends or new woman, leaving you with the day-to-day stress and drudgery to handle all by yourself.

Your youthful years—when you should be having fun and learning about yourself and the world, will instead be spent tied down with responsibility and obligation. As you struggle to put food on the table and keep the lights on, your anger and frustration will grow. But that's not all!

You will be passed over for a relationship by many great suitors . . . men that don't want to be bothered with raising some other guy's child. They don't want to have to play second fiddle to a child that isn't their own. However, you will be of major interest to pedophiles that know that lonely, overly trusting single mothers and their male-attention starved children are easy prey.

Many young women, so desperate for financial assistance and a break from parenting, set themselves up to become victims of guys that want instant commitment. They proclaim themselves to be in love very early in the relationship. Watch out for those that want to move in right away, promising to "help you" with bills you are desperate to pay.

Right now you have no clue about how depressed you will feel being stuck in the house week after week, taking care of a baby, changing smelly diapers, and wondering where your new boyfriend or "baby daddy" is tonight. You'll grow resentful at your responsibilities while your friends are going to college, enjoying parties and fabulous clothes, and creating a future for themselves as educated, influential women. You will be left behind.

Making Smart Choices

Take a moment and reflect on who you want to be and where you want to go in life. Every young woman can become a shining star and make all her dreams come true! But when you make poor decisions about who you allow to use your womb, you suffer a loss of opportunities and possibilities. When you make impulsive choices without thinking about the repercussions of your actions, your child suffers those repercussions right along with you.

The realization that you have messed up your life and have no one to blame for it but yourself will hit you sooner or later. When that moment arrives, keep your hands to yourself. Shaking, slapping, pinching, punching, body slamming, neglecting or killing your child in frustration and anger are criminal acts. Your baby didn't ask to be here—you chose that path. . . .

Right here, right now you have the opportunity to look into the future and make different choices for yourself. Begin by taking the time to plan your life and future goals. Children can be wonderful additions to your life plan, but should always be put AFTER educational accomplishment, career development and fiscal stability. Avoid making choices that will put you on a path to depression, poverty, or prison for 25 to life.

There is no need for you to have a baby when you are not married and have no one to help you love, care for and support that child's growth and development. Children should not just exist, but be born into an environment where their lives are enriched by their parents' love and devotion to their success.

Parenting a child is a two-person job best performed by a husband and wife. Why would you accept anything less for yourself or your child?

Viewpoint 2

> *"Could it be that once freed of the spousal system, fathers and mothers become better parents?"*

Single Parenting Can Be Beneficial

Sabrina Broadbent

In the following viewpoint, Sabrina Broadbent defends the ability of single parents to raise children. She puts forth that divorce can renew fathers and mothers damaged by failing marriages and bring closeness, availability, and support to parent-child relationships. Drawing from anecdotal experience, Broadbent also claims that children, including her own, have adjusted well to single-parent households and do not perceive themselves as disadvantaged. She even speculates that many two-parent homes are essentially run by single parents, with one responsible for rearing children and the other earning income. Broadbent is a British novelist and former English teacher.

As you read, consider the following questions:

1. According to Broadbent, how did her students with single parents describe their mothers and fathers?

Sabrina Broadbent, "When One Parent Is Better than Two," *Mail on Sunday*, July 19, 2009, p. 36.

2. How can staying together for the children lead to a more desperate scenario, in Broadbent's view?
3. What signs does Broadbent observe of growing equality between the sexes in parenting?

Among my group of friends, I was an early casualty in the battle of love and family life. My children's father and I separated when we were 40 and they were still at primary school, a stage when not many of us were doing divorce. It caused a bit of a stir. Yet ten years on, as we hit 50, a second wave of marital casualties is taking place. For once the chaos of family life receded, it seems that these parents found not peace but a sadness that would not go away. Was it worth staying together?

For too long we have believed that marriage is good, divorce is bad. Two parents are better than one. But what if single parenting is more harmonious and more loving than the conventional model? What if two-parent families are a bit of a lie, a shop front for what is in effect single parenting? What if it's wiser not to wait for Mr Right, but to have a child on your own?

I was an English teacher in London comprehensive schools for 20 years before the marking and the testing drove me out. In a Year 10 class last year [in 2008], we studied an article about 'Broken Britain', which described the damaging effects of divorce and single parenthood on the children in this country. The students were angry. They objected to the tone of the article and its references to 'poverty', 'low attainment', 'criminality' and 'despair'.

I was quite surprised. I asked everyone who lived in a single-parent household to stand up. Out of 25 teenagers, only two were left seated. I asked each person standing to say one thing that would counter the article's litany of gloom about single parents. A sea of hands rose. 'My mum is my role model—she works, she takes us to the cinema'; 'My dad makes me really proud. He cooks and helps with my homework'; 'It's easier since my parents separated. There's less tension'; 'My mum is my friend. I can tell her anything'; 'Before, it was them and us; now it doesn't feel like that—I feel promoted'.

Positive Parenting Behaviours

Far from considering themselves damaged and deprived by life with a single parent, these young people suggested a kind of family life and, in particular, a kind of relationship with their parent, about which most commentators and politicians seem unaware. They told of the renewal that divorce can bring, of positive parenting behaviours where there is closeness, listening, availability and support. What if, with the dissolution of the nuclear family structure, greater equality, intimacy and companionship develops between parent and children? Could it be that once freed of the spousal system, fathers and mothers become better parents?

Many married couples I knew watched appalled, from a safe distance, while my ex and I separated. No doubt many were thinking, 'There but for the grace of God go I.' Now that the dust has settled, I'm often asked by these people, 'And how are the children?' I sometimes think I detect in the searchlight sweep of their eyes an insatiable desire for lurid tales of adolescent meltdown—eating disorders, drug abuse or underage sex.

While not wanting to deny the sadness and pain my children felt, and sometimes still feel, about their parents' separation, my 17- and 15-year-old happen to be two of the sanest and most positive people I know. They don't swear at me or at strangers, they don't underachieve at school and they don't make a habit of staggering home at three in the morning—all of which is behaviour that other parents seem to consider normal in teenagers. What if it isn't? What if it is the acting out of unresolved conflicts between the parents or just poor parenting?

Choosing to Live in Poverty?

To be clear: the economic circumstances of most single parents are not caused by family form. . . . Most single parents cannot choose whether or not to live in poverty. The lack of choices is predetermined by a structure which penalizes these parents because of their status, and which refuses to recognize the legitimacy of any family other than a heterosexual, married, two-parent family. In addition, the difficulties suffered by many single-parent families simply expose more clearly the debilitating impact of conflicts between work and family responsibilities, conflicts that undermine all kinds of families.

Nancy E. Dowd,
In Defense of Single-Parent Families.
New York: New York University Press, 1997.

The Damage of Staying Together

Quantifying the damage of staying together for the children is rarely examined. In my 50s, it doesn't gladden me to witness a second wave of divorce among my married friends. Many of those parents who stayed together through the child-rearing years seem to have only delayed the inevitable. The children may be grown up but does that really make it a better time to call the whole thing off? Some might observe that the pain of separation for the adults at such a point is even more acute than when the love of family life consumes all one's attention. The staying-together-for-the-children scenario is more desperate if one of the parents has put their career on hold in order to raise the children, only to find that in their 50s they are unemployed and alone in an empty house. We hear a great deal, correctly, about the needs and rights of children. We should remember that parents are people too.

Raising children alone is tough, but what if it's not as tough as raising them in a two-parent household? And anyway, you may notice that the majority of two-parent households are to all intents and purposes a single-parent operation being run on archaic lines. Child rearing and running a home is left to one adult while the earning power, career advancement—and opportunity to get out when the going gets tough—is the preserve of the other.

I feel very lucky. I'm of that generation of women who may not have got our marriages right, but we did at least get pregnant while we were still relatively fertile. Even though the chances of staying with the father turned out to be compromised by conflicting expectations of domestic labour and careers, I thank God that I had my children when I did; they are the very best of both of us. I meet women in their 30s and 40s who ask, 'Should I give up waiting for a man and have a child?' I want to say, 'Do it. The chances are you'll be raising that child single-handedly whether you stay with the father or not. Just don't give up the day job.'

Growing Parity Between the Sexes

For my generation, who had children in the 1980s and 90s, the odds were perhaps stacked against us. I remember the shock, when I was pregnant with my first child in 1991, when I understood that not only would I have to return to work when she was 12 weeks old to keep my job and pay the mortgage, but that I was expected to pay for 50 hours of child care a week without any help from the state.

After a few months of struggle, it became obvious that financially we would be better off if I worked less. And so I went part-time. In many ways, those years were a precious gift of love and pleasure. It's only now, looking at my much depleted teacher's pension, halved because of those years, that I realise the gift was far from free.

In recent years, huge advances have been made with regard to maternity leave, paternity leave, child care, benefits and preschool education. These are making an incredible difference to the lives of children and their parents. I feel hopeful for my children. I have a feeling that by the time they have children of their own, there will be real parity between the sexes, not only at work but at home.

There are visible signs on the streets in the past five years—more men pushing buggies, men shopping with babies in slings, men on paternity leave and men working part-time. The other day I saw a man, laptop over one shoulder, nappy bag over the other, struggling on to the rush-hour tube with a baby in a buggy. Perhaps my daughters and their partners really will have it all—love, work and children. Now that would be something worth signing up to.

"If the claim is that same-sex parents are just as good as married biological parents, the statement is not supported by any substantial evidence and is almost certainly false."

Same-Sex Parenting Is Harmful

George W. Dent Jr.

George W. Dent Jr. is a law professor at Case Western Reserve University. In the following viewpoint, Dent writes that same-sex parenting is inferior to heterosexual parenting. Studies reporting that there is no difference between the two are unsatisfactory and are too small to be meaningful, according to Dent. He also maintains that in gay and lesbian households, children are denied biological ties with parents, subjected to increased instability and high rates of abuse, denied gender-specific nurturing from a mother or father, and are more likely to be confused about their own sexuality. Thus, Dent advises that same-sex marriage is not recognized, artificial reproduction is reserved for heterosexual married couples, and homosexual adoption is limited.

George W. Dent Jr., "No Difference? An Analysis of Same-Sex Parenting," 10 *Ave Maria L. Rev.* 53 (2011).

As you read, consider the following questions:

1. Why does the author scrutinize the fact that researchers have sought volunteers for same-sex parenting studies?
2. What conflicts do homosexual parents experience with parenting, as stated by Dent?
3. In what ways do the fragility of homosexual relationships affect children, as purported by the author?

The principal argument for traditional marriage is that it is uniquely beneficial to children. Accordingly, a key tenet of the campaign for same-sex marriage ("SSM") is that same-sex couples are just as good as other parents; there is "no difference" between the two. This [viewpoint] analyzes this claim and concludes that it is unsubstantiated and almost certainly false.

No Difference from What?

In *Perry v. Schwarzenegger* [also known as *Perry v. Brown*], the District Court pronounced that "same-sex parents and opposite-sex parents are of equal quality." Some scholars make similar claims. A crucial problem with the "no difference" claim is determining what is alleged to be no different from what. Defenders of traditional marriage claim that children generally fare best when raised by their married biological parents and (correlatively) that children would not fare as well with same-sex married couples.

Since SSM has been recognized only recently and only in a few jurisdictions, these claims cannot be empirically refuted or confirmed. In fact, no one has tried. In *Perry* the plaintiffs' expert witness could not identify any study comparing children raised by same-sex couples with children raised by their married biological parents. Studies of children raised by same-sex couples often compare them with children raised by single mothers. Others compare them to children raised by divorced heterosexual parents. Clearly neither comparison group does as well as children raised by their married biological parents, so on its face these claims carry little weight even if they are true.

Moreover, studies do suggest at least one significant difference of children raised by same-sex couples: They are more likely to engage in homosexuality and to experience greater confusion and anxiety about sex. Again, the absence of longitudinal data and of statistically significant samples mandates caution in weighing these findings. However, these new findings do raise suspicion that there may be other differences from same-sex parenting that have not yet been uncovered.

Other Methodological Problems

Most studies of same-sex parenting have small, self-selected samples of children who have not been in the household very long and who have been evaluated at a single time rather than followed for a substantial period. One researcher [Michael J. Rosenfeld] who clearly supports the gay movement concedes:

> [T]here has never been a comprehensive study of same-sex parents and their children from nationally representative data. . . . The studies that have been done on same-sex couples have been mostly small-scale studies of non-random samples from sampling frames that are not nationally representative.

This is not necessarily a result of any impropriety by the investigators. Until recently few examples of same-sex parenting existed (especially for gay male homes), so a large longitudinal study is not yet possible. Given the small number of children now being raised by same-sex couples, getting a statistically significant random sample would be extremely expensive; it would require looking at a very large random sample of children in order to get information about the one percent or so with same-sex couples. It is not surprising, then, that no one has done this.

Instead, researchers have sought volunteers to be studied. The validity of self-selected samples is doubtful. The legal guardians of children—of whatever sexual orientation or legal relationship—are unlikely to volunteer for a study if their children are not doing well. Also [according to Rosenfeld], "several of the most important [studies] have been based on samples of women who became parents through assisted reproductive technology," who tend to be "white, upper-middle class women." They may not be representative of the broader population.

Further, homosexual couples in these studies are intrepid pioneers, keenly aware of the obstacles they face. They would not take up the challenge of same-sex parenting unless they felt themselves able to conquer the difficulties and were determined to do so. In many social experiments such pioneers succeed, but less impressive people who later try the same thing do less well. Whatever the success of the pioneers of same-sex parenting has been, that success may not be matched by others in the future.

Finally, some studies find that children raised by their married biological parents fare best. They may then claim that this result stems from the "higher socioeconomic status" of these parents. That conclusion, however, raises the question of the direction of cause and effect. A classic justification for marriage is that having a wife and the presence or prospect of children motivates a man to earn more money and achieve higher status. Thus higher socioeconomic status of married couples may be a result of marriage.

For lack of evidence, especially about male couples and long-term effects, uncertainty about gay parenting will persist for years. Liberalization of divorce was touted on the seemingly humane premise that some marriages are irreparably broken and that it is better to let the parties end these marriages rather than to perpetuate their misery by forcing a couple either to stay married or to endure a long, bitter, damaging legal battle over questions of fault. It was argued that children would not be harmed by divorce because they are "infinitely malleable." [According to researcher Seana Sugrue,] "[I]t was fashionable among intellectuals to contend that the best interest of adults also serve the best interests of children. This once conventional wisdom has proven to be gravely mistaken. . . ."

The damage done to children by divorce became evident only many years after divorce laws were liberalized and divorce became more common. The experience with liberalized divorce follows the law of unintended consequences—major legal changes invariably produce unexpected effects. Likewise, an unprecedented change in the law and meaning of marriage may have detrimental consequences. The studies invoked by the gay movement cannot refute this possibility.

There is further empirical evidence and inductive reasons indicating that same-sex married couples almost certainly would not be equally good parents as are married biological parents.

Adoption vs. Biology. Every child with homosexual guardians has lost at least one biological parent. Loss of a parent is universally regarded as a great misfortune. If the child has one biological parent, the other adult is a stepparent. In fables stepparents are typically hostile to their stepchildren. Homosexual couples with children often experience competition or jealousy over parenting, and the children often have a preference for or "primary bond" with one parent. If one is the child's biological parent, it would be natural for the child to identify the other as secondary, or as not a true parent at all.

Alternatively, the child with homosexual custodians has lost both parents. This is universally regarded as a tragedy. Adoption can be a great blessing for children whose parents are unable or unwilling to care for them, but even adoption by a traditional married couple is not equal to the biological family. If same-sex couples are just as good as biological par-

Wanting a 'Normal' Mother

I built up a great deal of fear and frustration. I was angry that I was not part of a 'normal' family and could not live with a 'normal' mother. I wondered what I did to deserve this. Why did my biological mother let a lesbian adopt me? How could she think that this life was better than what she could have given me?. . . During these years I talked with my sister about my feelings and problems. We discussed how we didn't understand my mother and her lifestyle. We talked of how we resented her for placing us in such a situation, all the while knowing how hard it would be for us.

Carey Conley,
"Always Changes," in Different Mothers: Sons and Daughters of Lesbians Talk About Their Lives,
ed. Louise Rafkin. Pittsburgh, PA: Cleis Press, 1990.

ents, they must be *better* than traditional married couples as adoptive parents. It would be astounding if this were true, and there is no evidence to suggest that it is.

Adopted children often crave knowledge of and contact with their biological parents and are challenging laws that prevent them from having it. In effect, these children assert the natural importance of blood ties and a human right to access to their biological parents. The law increasingly acknowledges such a right. The [United Nations] Convention on the Rights of the Child, for example, recognizes the right of every child, "as far as possible . . . to know and be cared for by his or her parents." Because homosexual couples cannot biologically create children, however, the SSM movement must deny the importance of blood ties and any right of children to access to their biological parents.

Special Issues with Same-Sex Couples. In addition to the detriments of adoption even by a traditional married couple, there are reasons to believe that adoption by same-sex couples would raise further problems.

1. Children's Sexuality

The claim that living with a same-sex couple does not affect a child's sexuality is implausible. "It would be surprising indeed if . . . children's own sexual identities were unaffected by the sexual identities of their parents" [according to researcher Diana Baumrind]. Even young children may sense, or be told by others, that their guardians are unusual—queer—thereby initiating their sexualization at an unusually early age. There is evidence that children raised by homosexuals are more likely to engage in homosexuality and to feel confused about their sexual identity.

2. Durability and Fidelity

Other aspects of homosexual relationships make same-sex couples less likely to be good parents. Heterosexual relationships are more durable. The bond between woman and man is rooted in the biological necessity to nurture human infants for a long time. The parents' fidelity affirms paternity—the identity of the father—which is hidden by promiscuity in some other species, including close relatives of humans, like chimpanzees. The recognition of paternity lets a father care for his own children, which includes caring for their mother—his mate. . . . For either parent to have sex outside the marriage can disrupt their bond by creating competing demands from other children and the other parent(s).

It would be astonishing if this natural bond, a product of a million years of evolution, were just coincidentally equaled by the bond between same-sex couples, which has no biological basis. A comparison with other species is instructive. Among some animals male and female mate for life; among many they do not. But in no species do members of the same sex mate for life. Homosexuals have less reason to bond as couples and, when they do bond, less reason for the bond to be enduring and exclusive. Not surprisingly, then, homosexuals are less inclined than heterosexuals to marry, and gays who do marry have a high divorce rate.

Where homosexuals (especially gay men) do marry or otherwise enter into a committed relationship, it generally happens later in life than it generally does for normal couples. This is not surprising. A normal motive for a traditional marriage is to start a family, so it generally occurs when the couple is young enough to bear children and to handle the physical rigors of raising them. Gay couples do not bear children. Further, [according to researcher Judith Stacey] "gay men tend to be even more preoccupied than most straight women with their bodies, physical attractiveness, attire, adornment and self-presentation." They may choose to marry only when they no longer feel attractive enough for the promiscuity of the homosexual "meat market." . . .

Given the fragility of homosexual relationships, children in these homes are more likely to suffer the stresses of divorce and to learn that marriage is temporary, not a lasting relationship of trust. Every child raised by a homosexual couple has already lost at least one biological parent, so a divorce may cause heightened trauma. Given the frequent infidelity in homosexual couples, children in these homes are more likely to witness conflict over infidelity and to see it as a normal part of marriage. Given the frequent violence in homosexual couples, children in these homes are more likely to witness domestic violence and to understand it as a normal part of marriage.

A child whose mother lives with a man other than his biological father is more likely to be abused by that man than a child living with his biological father is likely to be abused by him. Every child raised by a gay male couple has at least one unrelated male adult in the home. There is no reason to think that such a child will fare better than a child living with an unrelated heterosexual male. The high rates of child sex abuse among homosexuals and bisexuals are also a cause for concern. At the least, given the uncertain effects of homosexual parenting, the children raised by homosexual couples are being treated as guinea pigs, which is troubling.

3. Parents and Gender

Advocates of same-sex parenting claim there is no difference between having a mother and a father and having two guardians of the same sex. This, too, is implausible. Men and women differ in significant ways.... [According to child psychologist Dr. Kyle Pruett,] "Fathers tend to do things differently, but not in ways that are worse for the children. Fathers do not mother, they father." The contribution of fathers benefits their children. The presence of fathers in the home also benefits the neighborhoods where they live.

Because of problems like these, "the American College of Pediatricians believes it is inappropriate, potentially hazardous to children, and dangerously irresponsible to change the age-old prohibition on homosexual parenting, whether by adoption, foster care, or by reproductive manipulation." Most European countries bar adoption by gays and lesbians. A complete prohibition on adoption or foster care by homosexual couples would be inappropriate. In war-torn, impoverished countries there are starving orphans who would be better off if they were adopted by carefully screened homosexual couples. However, adoption by homosexual couples should be limited, requiring a showing that no better placement is possible.

Same-Sex Couples and Artificial Reproduction

Not surprisingly, some homosexuals are using artificial means of reproduction. Recognition of SSM arguably requires that artificial reproduction (including cloning) be legalized. Since homosexuals cannot create children sexually, the principle of equality arguably entitles them to other means of reproducing. This argument has already been accepted in some countries that have validated SSM.

Artificial reproduction generally entails the separation of the resulting child from one or both of its biological parents. To plan deliberately to separate a child from one or both parents seems to be child abuse. At least in theory, biological parents can act in their own interests; infant or unborn children cannot. Although baby selling is illegal, adults can give or take pay for egg or sperm donations or surrogate motherhood and take steps to prevent the resulting children from having any legal rights against, or contact with, or even knowledge of the identity of their parents. In this way some men have sired hundreds of children.

Artificial reproduction is more problematic than adoption because the former is harder for the law to monitor. Every adoption must be approved by a court charged to protect the child. Artificial reproduction gets little legal oversight. The children created are subject to the whims of adults. Artificial reproduction also differs from adoption in that the former is irreversible. If an adoption goes awry it can be rescinded, but the artificial creation of a human being cannot be undone. Neither artificially created children nor adoptees have an adequate natural family to which they can return. The difference between the two is that for the artificially created child this happens by the design of the custodial parents.

The law has paid little attention to the rights of children regarding their biological parents because in the past there was no threat to these rights. Children lived with their natural parents unless the parents died, voluntarily surrendered them, or were found unfit by a court. Through artificial reproduction children may be separated from their biological parents without any of these conditions being present. This separation damages children. Children artificially conceived and raised apart from their biological fathers "hunger for an abiding paternal presence" [according to Pruett].

Changing a Fundamental Institution

The claim that there is "no difference" between homosexual and heterosexual parents is ambiguous. If it means that same-sex couples are as good as single parents, the statement may be true, but it is largely irrelevant to the debate over same-sex marriage where the issue is whether SSM is just as good as traditional marriage. If the claim is that same-sex parents are just as good as married biological parents, the statement is not supported by any substantial evidence and is almost certainly false. Empirical studies indicate some problems with same-sex parenting, and inductive reasons give further cause for concern.

Supporters of SSM want to change marriage—an institution that has been fundamental in every culture in every corner of the globe throughout history—in a way that, with a few recent exceptions, has never been tried before. Minimal prudence forbids such a radical change until we have strong evidence that it will do no harm. In other words, the burden of proof should be on advocates of SSM. They cannot sustain that burden now, and it [is] unlikely that they will ever be able to do so because only traditional marriage is rooted in human nature. Accordingly, same-sex marriage should not be recognized by law, artificial reproduction should be permitted only to traditional married couples, and adoption by same-sex couples should be allowed only in limited circumstances.

"In some ways, gay parents may bring talents to the table that straight parents don't."

Same-Sex Parenting Is Beneficial

Stephanie Pappas

In the following viewpoint, Stephanie Pappas proposes that not only do children raised by same-sex couples fare as well as those raised by heterosexual couples, but also that gay parenting offers several advantages. Gay and lesbian parents may be more committed and motivated than heterosexual parents, considering the accidental birth rate, she claims. Pappas continues that same-sex couples are more likely to adopt children who linger in the foster system, such as minorities and kids who are older or have special needs. Additionally, gay and lesbian parents, she suggests, provide a unique environment that promotes open-mindedness, tolerance, and gender equality. Pappas is a senior writer for LiveScience, a science news website.

As you read, consider the following questions:

1. What statistics does Pappas offer to support her position that gay and lesbian parents tend to adopt more children in need?

Stephanie Pappas, "Why Gay Parents May Be the Best Parents," LiveScience.com, January 15, 2012.

2. How does Judith Stacey follow up on her claim that the research on parenting is misrepresented by people who advocate children needing both a father and mother?
3. What is the disadvantage of same-sex parenting, as argued by Brian Powell?

Gay marriage, and especially gay parenting, has been in the crosshairs in recent days.

On Jan. 6 [2012], Republican presidential hopeful Rick Santorum told a New Hampshire audience that children are better off with a father in prison than being raised in a home with lesbian parents and no father at all. And last Monday (Jan. 9), Pope Benedict called gay marriage a threat "to the future of humanity itself," citing the need for children to have heterosexual homes.

But research on families headed by gays and lesbians doesn't back up these dire assertions. In fact, in some ways, gay parents may bring talents to the table that straight parents don't.

Gay parents "tend to be more motivated, more committed than heterosexual parents on average, because they chose to be parents," said Abbie Goldberg, a psychologist at Clark University in Massachusetts who researches gay and lesbian parenting. Gays and lesbians rarely become parents by accident, compared with an almost 50 percent accidental pregnancy rate among heterosexuals, Goldberg said. "That translates to greater commitment on average and more involvement."

And while research indicates that kids of gay parents show few differences in achievement, mental health, social functioning and other measures, these kids may have the advantage of open-mindedness, tolerance and role models for equitable relationships, according to some research. Not only that, but gays and lesbians are likely to provide homes for difficult-to-place children in the foster system, studies show. (Of course, this isn't to say that heterosexual parents can't bring these same qualities to the parenting table.)

Adopting the Neediest

Gay adoption recently caused controversy in Illinois, where Catholic Charities adoption services decided in November to cease offering services because the state refused funding unless the groups agreed not to discriminate against gays and lesbians. Rather than comply, Catholic Charities closed up shop.

Catholic opposition aside, research suggests that gay and lesbian parents are actually a powerful resource for kids in need of adoption. According to a 2007 report by the Williams Institute and the Urban Institute, 65,000 kids were living with adoptive gay parents between 2000 and 2002, with another 14,000 in foster homes headed by gays and lesbians. (There are currently more than 100,000 kids in foster care in the U.S.)

An October 2011 report by the Evan B. Donaldson Adoption Institute found that, of gay and lesbian adoptions at more than 300 agencies, 10 percent of the kids placed were older than 6—typically a very difficult age to adopt out. About 25 percent were older than 3. Sixty percent of gay and lesbian couples adopted across races, which is important given that minority children in the foster system tend to linger. More than half of the kids adopted by gays and lesbians had special needs.

The report didn't compare the adoption preferences of gay couples directly with those of heterosexual couples, said author David Brodzinsky, research director at the institute and co-editor of *Adoption by Lesbians and Gay Men: A New Dimension of Family Diversity* (Oxford University Press, 2011). But research suggests that gays and lesbians are more likely than heterosexuals to adopt older, special needs and minority children, he said. Part of that could be their own preferences, and part could be because of discrimination by adoption agencies that puts more difficult children with what caseworkers see as "less desirable" parents.

No matter how you slice it, Brodzinsky told LiveScience, gays and lesbians are highly interested in adoption as a group. The 2007 report by the Urban Institute also found that more than half of gay men and 41 percent of lesbians in the U.S. would like to adopt. That adds up to an estimated 2 million gay people who are interested in adoption. It's a huge reservoir of potential parents who could get kids out of the instability of the foster system, Brodzinsky said.

"When you think about the 114,000 children who are freed for adoption who continue to live in foster care and who are not being readily adopted, the goal is to increase the pool of available, interested and well-trained individuals to parent these children," Brodzinsky said.

In addition, Brodzinsky said there's evidence to suggest that gays and lesbians are especially accepting of open adoptions, where the child retains some contact with his or her birth parents. And the statistics bear out that birth parents often have no problem with their kids being raised by same-sex couples, he added.

"Interestingly, we find that a small percentage, but enough to be noteworthy, [of birth mothers] make a conscious decision to place with gay men, so they can be the only mother in their child's life," Brodzinsky said.

Good Parenting

Research has shown that the kids of same-sex couples—both adopted and biological kids—fare no worse than the kids of straight couples on mental health, social functioning, school performance and a variety of other life-success measures.

In a 2010 review of virtually every study on gay parenting, New York University sociologist Judith Stacey and University of Southern California sociologist Tim Biblarz found no dif-

Committed Homosexual Parents

While gays have higher rates of promiscuity and relationship infidelity than do heterosexuals, it is unlikely that this would be equally true for homosexual couples who were parenting in the context of marriage or civil unions. Recent data, for instance, indicates that forty-one percent of lesbigay [lesbian, bisexual, and gay] parents raising children have been together for five years or longer as compared to only twenty percent of heterosexual unmarried couples. The normalization of lesbigay relationships through the legalization of same-sex marriage, and particularly child rearing in the context of these committed relationships, would likely promote fidelity in lesbigay relationships, just as it does in heterosexual relationships.

Richard E. Redding, "It's Really About Sex: Same-Sex Marriage, Lesbigay Parenting, and the Psychology of Disgust," Duke Journal of Gender Law & Policy, *vol. 15:127, 2008.*

ferences between children raised in homes with two heterosexual parents and children raised with lesbian parents.

"There's no doubt whatsoever from the research that children with two lesbian parents are growing up to be just as well adjusted and successful as children with a male and a female parent," Stacey told LiveScience.

There is very little research on the children of gay men, so Stacey and Biblarz couldn't draw conclusions on those families. But Stacey suspects that gay men "will be the best parents on average," she said.

That's a speculation, she said, but if lesbian parents have to really plan to have a child, it's even harder for gay men. Those who decide to do it are thus likely to be extremely committed, Stacey said. Gay men may also experience fewer parenting conflicts, she added. Most lesbians use donor sperm to have a child, so one mother is biological and the other is not, which could create conflict because one mother may feel closer to the kid.

"With gay men, you don't have that factor," she said. "Neither of them gets pregnant, neither of them breast-feeds, so you don't have that asymmetry built into the relationship."

The bottom line, Stacey said, is that people who say children need both a father and a mother in the home are misrepresenting the research, most of which compares children of single parents to children of married couples. Two good parents are better than one good parent, Stacey said, but one good parent is better than two bad parents. And gender seems to make no difference. While you do find broad differences between how men and women parent on average, she said, there is much more diversity within the genders than between them.

"Two heterosexual parents of the same educational background, class, race and religion are more like each other in the way they parent than one is like all other women and one is like all other men," she said.

Nurturing Tolerance

In fact, the only consistent places you find differences between how kids of gay parents and kids of straight parents turn out are in issues of tolerance and open-mindedness, according to Goldberg. In a paper published in 2007 in the *American Journal of Orthopsychiatry*, Goldberg conducted in-depth interviews with 46 adults with at least one gay parent. Twenty-eight of them spontaneously offered that they felt more open-minded and empathetic than people not raised in their situation.

"These individuals feel like their perspectives on family, on gender, on sexuality have largely been enhanced by growing up with gay parents," Goldberg said.

One 33-year-old man with a lesbian mother told Goldberg, "I feel I'm a more open, well-rounded person for having been raised in a nontraditional family, and I think those that know me would agree. My mom opened me up to the positive impact of differences in people."

Children of gay parents also reported feeling less stymied by gender stereotypes than they would have been if raised in straight households. That's likely because gays and lesbians tend to have more egalitarian relationships than straight couples, Goldberg said. They're also less wedded to rigid gender stereotypes themselves.

"Men and women felt like they were free to pursue a wide range of interests," Goldberg said. "Nobody was telling them, 'Oh, you can't do that, that's a boy thing,' or 'That's a girl thing.'"

Same-Sex Acceptance

If same-sex marriage does disadvantage kids in any way, it has nothing to do with their parents' gender and everything to do with society's reaction toward the families, said Indiana University sociologist Brian Powell, the author of *Counted Out: Same-Sex Relations and Americans' Definitions of Family*.

"Imagine being a child living in a state with two parents in which, legally, only one parent is allowed to be their parent," Powell told LiveScience. "In that situation, the family is not seen as authentic or real by others. That would be the disadvantage."

In her research, Goldberg has found that many children of gay and lesbian parents say that more acceptance of gay and lesbian families, not less, would help solve this problem.

In a study published online Jan. 11, 2012, in the *Journal of Marriage and Family*, Goldberg interviewed another group of

49 teenagers and young adults with gay parents and found that not one of them rejected the right of gays and lesbians to marry. Most cited legal benefits as well as social acceptance.

"I was just thinking about this with a couple of friends and just was in tears thinking about how different my childhood might have been had same-sex marriage been legalized 25 years ago," a 23-year-old man raised by a lesbian couple told Goldberg. "The cultural, legal status of same-sex couples impacts the family narratives of same-sex families—how we see ourselves in relation to the larger culture, whether we see ourselves as accepted or outsiders."

VIEWPOINT 5

"The characteristics of the teens that fall into the pattern of teen births mean they are probably the hardest to reach and those more deeply entrenched in a culture and a reality of teens having children."

Teen Parenting Is Harmful

Schuyler Center for Analysis and Advocacy

In the following viewpoint, the Schuyler Center for Analysis and Advocacy (SCAA) states that teen parenting has negative consequences for both the children and young parents. Children born to adolescent mothers face numerous disadvantages such as poverty, lower academic performance, social behavior problems, and even high risks of teen pregnancy and incarceration. Teen parenting is also associated with family and social instability, which can result in homelessness and burden to the child welfare system. The SCAA, based in Albany, New York, is an advocacy group for low-income and vulnerable populations.

As you read, consider the following questions:

1. As claimed by the SCAA, how do children born of mothers seventeen and younger begin kindergarten?

"Teenage Births: Outcomes for Young Parents and Their Children," Schuyler Center for Analysis and Advocacy, December 2008.

2. How can depression caused by adolescent motherhood affect parenting, as described by the SCAA?
3. According to the viewpoint, in what ways does teen parenthood significantly cut into state resources?

Fortunately, the number of teen mothers is declining across the United States. The decline is evident across all states, ethnicities and racial groups although teens in minority groups and those living in low-income communities remain at higher risk. . . .

Poverty: Both a Cause and a Result of Teen Childbearing

Research demonstrates that childbearing during the teen years is both a result and cause of poverty. The same complicated set of socioeconomic factors that puts teenagers at risk of childbearing also contributes to the reality that teen parents continue to live in poverty. These are teens with less education, members of racial and ethnic minority groups, and those who live in communities with high rates of both poverty and nonmarital births. While it is true that some children will be raised in poverty regardless of the age of their parents when they were born, teenage childbearing perpetuates the liability of poverty on the mother and the child.

According to research [by J. Frost and others], "A greater proportion of young women who are poor become sexually active as adolescents, do not use a contraceptive method at first intercourse and give birth by age 20." These youth also have "lower self-efficacy in obtaining and using contraceptives effectively."

Compared to mothers just ten years older, teen mothers are almost three times as likely to require some sort of public assistance. Waiting just a few years to have children can reduce the odds of living in poverty by almost 20%. In New York, teen mothers are far more likely to live in poverty than their nonparent peers. . . .

Educational Achievement and Social Development

The consequences of teen childbearing are reflected in the lower educational achievements of both the mothers and children. Making up for the lost time and reduced opportunities afforded to these groups is costly and time-consuming.

Of the 63,000 high school dropouts in New York in 2006, it is safe to say that some were teen parents—both mothers and fathers. Pregnancy can complicate the school experience. Expectant mothers may need to deal with stigma and unwanted attention. New parents have less time for their studies and for sleep. They must also handle adult responsibilities they are not ready or equipped for, including juggling complex child care schedules and providing child support. Many must work to support themselves and their baby. None of these complications are conducive to completing school, and either continuing their education or starting a career.

Teen Mothers

- Nearly one in three girls cited pregnancy as the reason they dropped out of school in 2004.
- Even after controlling for race, economic status, and other characteristics, having a child before the age of 20 reduces academic attainment by almost three years.
- Only 63% of teenagers who give birth before age 18 either graduate from high school or receive their GED [general equivalency diploma] as compared to 85% of women who delay childbirth until their early twenties.
- Only 5% of young teen mothers complete at least two years of college by age 30 and less than 2% obtain a college degree.

While parenting is difficult for teens, their children are starting life at a distinct disadvantage. Their parents probably lack life experience, skills, maturity, and economic security. Chances are the pregnancy derailed the parents' education and life plans. In other cases the parents were already disconnected from their future. Supports such as home visiting and parent education are important in order to break what could become a cycle of adverse outcomes visited on both the teen parents and their child.

Children of Teen Mothers

- Children born to mothers ages 17 and younger begin kindergarten with lower levels of school readiness, including lower math and reading scores, language and communication skills, social skills and physical and emotional well-being, than children of older mothers. Children born to mothers ages 18–19 do not perform much better on most measures.
- Children of teen mothers are 50% more likely than children of older parents to repeat a grade, are less likely to complete high school than the children of older mothers, and have lower performance on standardized tests.
- Children of teen mothers are more likely to be unemployed and to become teenage parents themselves than those born to women who delay childbearing.
- Children born to teen mothers are at greater risk of social behavioral problems and are almost three times as likely to be incarcerated during their adolescence or early 20s as are the children of older mothers....

Mental Health of Teen Mothers. The importance of adolescent mental health has often been overlooked by the medical community, educators, policy makers and even parents. An estimated 40,000 youth between the ages of 14–18 receive inpatient or outpatient mental health treatment in any given year in New York State but evidence suggests that many more remain undiagnosed or untreated. Adolescent motherhood can increase the risk of mental health problems, including depression that reduces the ability to form attachments, interferes with attentiveness and nurturing, and results in disengagement from the child.

Stress can also take a toll on a teen mother and her children—physically, mentally and emotionally. For example, one study found that high levels of hormones produced when under stress were associated with lower fetal weight. Data from the New York State Pregnancy Risk Assessment Monitoring System (PRAMS) database show that teen mothers suffer from a number of stress factors including relocation, arguments with partner, physical altercations, and death or illness of family members.

Family Stability

Stable family and social relationships are critical to ameliorating some of the accumulated disadvantages—greater risk for poor economic, health and educational outcomes—associated with teen mothers and their children. Family stability and support has a great influence on the health and welfare of the mother and the child.

Homelessness. Five percent of all teen mothers reported that they were homeless at the time they gave birth. In New York, over 1,252 teens with 694 children sought shelter in a facility for runaway and homeless youth in 2005.

Research on households headed by teenage mothers living in homeless shelters in New York City revealed similar troubling statistics:

- In 2003, almost half of homeless heads of household in shelters were teenage mothers. One-third were homeless before age 18 and 42% had been homeless more than once.
- 41% of the teen mothers in homeless shelters were removed from parental care; 39% witnessed domestic violence as a child and 25% were abused as children. A little over half were born to teenage mothers themselves.
- Children born into homeless families headed by teen mothers were three times more likely to be homeless more than once (17% vs. 6%); the children were 60% more likely to be removed from parental care (16% vs. 10%) and virtually none of them received any emotional or financial support from their absentee fathers.

Young women and their children in the shelter system are without the supports necessary to keep them in either their parents' homes or their own. They most likely left those homes due to conflict, domestic abuse, or poverty. Once homeless, every effort must be made to reconnect these young mothers with the social services necessary to get them back on their feet and, maybe more importantly, connected to a caring adult who can lend support.

Child Welfare. The consequences of an unstable home life are evident in data around teen births to girls in foster care. Teens in foster care are likely to suffer from maltreatment; in addition, once teens "age out" of foster care at age 18, there are few supports available to them. It is estimated that teen childbearing costs the child welfare system $2 billion a year. . . .

No Quick Fixes

The data and information in this [viewpoint] clearly show the complexity of the causes and consequences of teenage childbearing. While it is generally acknowledged that teen mothers and their children are more likely to live in poverty and require various forms of public assistance, the broader effects on their lives are not always understood.

When viewed across the spectrum of life, the consequences of teen births are staggering. Just the lost potential of the mothers and children coupled with the amount of money expended on health, mental health, child welfare, food and nutrition programs, economic security and numerous other programs cut significantly into state resources. According to one analysis, teen childbearing cost New York State $421 million in 2004 alone.

Then there are the human costs: children suffering from abuse and neglect, children born with physical or developmental problems because they were [of a low birth weight], children who grow up at an increased risk of incarceration or of becoming teen parents themselves. There are also the mothers who quit school and remain in low-wage jobs, and the fathers whose earnings never reach their potential because they started paying child support so early in their own lives.

Research suggests that there are no quick fixes. The characteristics of the teens that fall into the pattern of teen births mean they are probably the hardest to reach and those more deeply entrenched in a culture and a reality of teens having children.

Viewpoint 

> *"Teenage parenting may be more of an opportunity than a catastrophe."*

Teen Parenting Can Be Beneficial

Simon Duncan, Rosalind Edwards, and Claire Alexander

Simon Duncan, Rosalind Edwards, and Claire Alexander are authors of Teenage Parenthood: What's the Problem? *In the following viewpoint excerpted from* Teenage Parenthood, *they contend that teenage parenting can be a positive experience for young women and men, children, and society. Contrary to how teenage parenting is commonly understood, the authors contend it often is not a consequence of irresponsibility or low expectations, and they propose that many teenage pregnancies are planned, or if unplanned, not necessarily unwanted. Furthermore, they add, becoming a parent can help improve family relationships, provide meaningful purpose to people's lives, and be an impetus to educational or profession change. Nonetheless, policies for teenage parenting anticipate only negative outcomes and are unhelpful, maintain the authors.*

Simon Duncan, Rosalind Edwards, and Claire Alexander, "What's the Problem with Teenage Parents?," *Teenage Parenthood: What's the Problem?*, Tufnell Press, 2010, pp. 1–4, 9, 11–13, 15–16.

As you read, consider the following questions:

1. According to the authors, how does the downplaying and undervaluing of caring for families shape the discourse on teen parenting?
2. As stated in the viewpoint, what does US research reveal about the social outcomes of the mother's age at birth as a factor in parenting?
3. As explained by the authors, how does the research contradict assumptions about teenage fathers?

On 13th February 2009, the front page of the *Sun* newspaper carried the headline, 'Dad at 13'.[1] Alongside a full-page photograph of 'baby-faced father' Alfie Patten, with his newborn daughter, Maisie, the story told of the baby's birth to Alfie, aged thirteen, and Chantelle, aged fifteen, 'after just one night of unprotected sex'. The paper quoted Chantelle: 'We know we made a mistake but I wouldn't change it now. We will be good loving parents . . . I'll be a great mum and Alfie will be a great dad'. *Sun* columnist Jane Moore was more sceptical, dismissing their aspirations as 'heartbreakingly naïve', blaming both the failure of sex education in schools and the declining moral values of society—'the thin end of a wedge that will break the existing cracks in society so wide open that there'll be no hope of repair'. Over the following weekend, a storm of moral condemnation and outrage grew throughout the print and TV media and from politicians across the political spectrum. In the press, the focus—and the blame—settled squarely on the 'underclass' family background of the young parents, with the *Daily Express* commenting:

> You only have to take a look at their parents to see where it all went wrong. Imagine everyone's surprise that Chantelle's

1. After a DNA test, Alfie was later found not to be the father, which reportedly left him "extremely distressed." *Times Online*, May 19, 2009.

> parents live on benefits and, despite her dad being jobless, have six children. Alfie, meanwhile, is the son of a single mother and a father who's fathered no fewer than nine children . . . a world of broken homes and benefits, where irresponsibility and fecklessness reign supreme.

The *Sunday Times* similarly saw the event as a symbol of a Britain in moral decline and symptomatic of the growth of an underclass living parasitically on the welfare system—something, they argued that the country could ill-afford in a time of recession:

> Britain is doing low-life better than almost all other developed countries. A growing segment, which [American social policy analyst] Charles Murray . . . called the underclass, is devoid of the values and morality of a civilised society which foolishly provides the financial incentives to behave badly. . . . As each generation moves further away from family stability, we lumber ourselves with the enormous cost of propping up failed families and living with the social consequences. It is a grim prospect, especially as the country moves into deeper recession. . . .

A Severe Problem with the Public View

The reaction to the story of Alfie and Chantelle, like these earlier stories, points to a broader set of discourses around teenage parenting that consistently mark out the media and political responses to this issue. First, there is the taking of what are extreme and untypical cases as representative, and as a lens through which the broader social issue of teenage parenting might be understood. Second, there is the construction of teenage mothering as a uniformly negative experience for the mothers themselves, their children and for society as a whole. Third, there is the linking of teenage parenting with moral and cultural breakdown, placing children, parents and extended families beyond the pale of 'civilised society'. In this way teenage parents are positioned in some assumed 'underclass' where teenage mothers are commonly portrayed as ignorant and irresponsible, or even immoral, and young fathers are pictured as feckless. Both may be criminal. In this way the public discourse about teenage parenting has become conflated with a wider social threat discourse about the decline of marriage, single parenting, and teenage sexuality. Finally, there is the conflation of social problems with economic costs, most particularly around the supposed 'benefits culture' that 'encourages' young women to get pregnant at the expense of the rest of society. Tony Kerridge, of Marie Stopes International, was thus quoted:

> We have got the social aspect of young girls in the UK seeing having a baby as a route to getting their own place. These sorts of lifestyle choices can be dealt with on an educational level if teenage girls realise what they are contemplating is a route into social deprivation and being in the benefits culture for the rest of their lives.

Indeed, the idea of 'cost'—moral, social and economic—appears to stand at the heart of the issue of teenage parenting, and points to the prevailing concern, in the media, politics and policy, with an overwhelmingly individualistic and econometric model of the good mother/father, the good family, and the good citizen. In this view the ability to work, to earn and to pay are assumed as the primary prerequisites of social participation and recognition. Caring for others in families and communities is downplayed and undervalued. What seems axiomatic in this discourse is that teenage parents are necessarily and incontrovertibly *bad people, bad parents* and *bad citizens*, condemned to a lifetime of poverty, social handouts and economic apathy, and destined to repeat these failures across the generations. In this way the issue of teenage parenting, as presented publicly, combines a potent fusion of moral and economic crisis, of cultural and social dysfunction, wrapped in the virtuous certainties of impending disaster.

There is a severe problem with this 'public', axiomatic view of teenage parenting, however—the evidence does not support it.... There is little evidence that lack of knowledge 'causes' pregnancy, or that increased knowledge prevents it. Teenage birth rates are much lower than in the 1960s and 1970s, and overall are continuing to decline, while few teenage mothers are under sixteen. Age at which pregnancy occurs seems to have little effect on future social outcomes (like employment and income in later life), or on current levels of disadvantage for either parents or their children. Many young mothers and fathers themselves express positive attitudes to parenthood, and mothers usually describe how motherhood makes them feel stronger, more competent, more connected, and more responsible. Many fathers seek to remain connected to their children, and provide for their new family. For many young mothers and fathers parenting seems to provide the impetus to change direction, or build on existing resources, so as to take up education, training and employment. Teenage parenting may be more of an opportunity than a catastrophe....

Unfounded Assumptions About Teen Parents

The perceived social threat from teenage parenting is buttressed by a negative public consensus around teenage conception and pregnancy itself. This consensus assumes that teenage pregnancy is increasing rapidly, that this increase is particularly marked among younger teenagers, that all teenage pregnancies are unplanned, that all these unplanned conceptions are unwanted, and that new teenage mothers are inevitably also single mothers without stable relationships with partners. All these assumptions are unfounded, but all serve to bolster the negative evaluation of subsequent teenage parenting, and hence the nature of the policy response....

Whatever the level of teenage pregnancy, it is assumed in the public and media discourse that all teenage pregnancies are unplanned, that all unplanned conceptions are unwanted, and that most result from ignorance if not willful immorality. Certainly the Social Exclusion Unit's framework 1999 report identified 'ignorance'—the 'lack of accurate knowledge about contraception, STIs (sexually transmitted infections), what to expect in relationships and what it means to be a parent'—as major cause of teenage pregnancy. This is repeated in succeeding policy and guidance documents. But there is little support for the assumption that teenage parents are particularly ignorant about sex, contraception and parenting; that low levels of knowledge 'cause' teenage pregnancy; or that increased knowledge reduces pregnancy. It is hard to find young mothers who become pregnant due to ignorance about sex and contraception. Similarly, a meta-analysis of preventative strategies focusing on sex education, and improved access to advice and contraceptive services, concluded that this did not reduce unintended pregnancies among young women aged between 11–18.

Indeed a significant minority of teenage mothers, and fathers, positively plan for pregnancy. Some are hoping for birthing success after an earlier miscarriage, others in this group, especially those with partners, plan for subsequent children so as to complete their desired family size and hence 'build' a family. Many other teenage parents are 'positively ambivalent' towards childbirth—that is they do not actually plan it, but would quite like a baby and do not use contraception for that reason. For most teenage parents pregnancy may well be 'unplanned', but then so are many, if not most, pregnancies for all women—the very idea of 'planning pregnancy' is something of a grey area to say the least. Few teenage mothers, it seems, regret early childbirth. . . . As with other women 'unplanned' pregnancy does not necessarily mean 'unwanted' pregnancy for teenage parents. . . .

Poverty Is Not Caused by Early Childbearing

Americans must ask themselves what, realistically, they want teenagers to do. Should young women postpone childbearing until society deems them fit for parenthood? Should they simply get married, and run the risk of winding up financially worse off if they divorce? Or should early childbearing be seen as a young woman's response, limited and at times self-defeating, to the racial, class, and gender barriers in her life? Americans have every right to be concerned about early childbearing and to place the issue high on the national agenda. But they should think of it as a *measure*, not a cause, of poverty and other social ills. A teenager who has a baby usually adds but a slight burden to her life, which is already profoundly disadvantaged. Tempting as it may be to imagine that poverty is largely a result of teenagers' "untimely" choices, the data simply do not bear this out. Early childbearing may make a bad situation worse, but the real causes of poverty lie elsewhere.

Kristin Luker,
Dubious Conceptions: The Politics of Teenage Pregnancy.
Cambridge, MA: Harvard University Press, 1996.

Social Disadvantage vs. Teenage Mothering

The influential UNICEF [United Nations Children's Fund] report "Teenage Births in Rich Nations" claims that:

> giving birth as a teenager is believed to be bad for the young mother because the statistics suggest that she is much more likely to drop out of school, to have low or no qualifications, to be unemployed or low paid, to grow up without a

father, to become a victim of neglect and abuse, to do less well at school, to become involved in crime, use drugs and alcohol.

But in fact the statistics show nothing of the sort—if we deal with the errors committed by statements like these. For the statement does not compare like with like in reaching its 'much more likely' attribution of statistical causation; ascribing causal effects to teenage motherhood is pretty meaningless if we compare teenage mothers with all mothers, rather than those of a similar background. Rather, if we wish to measure the statistical effect of teenage motherhood (and then go on to ascribe a social effect, which is not necessarily the same thing) we need to control for variation in other variables, so that we do compare like with like. In more formal terms, statistical analysis needs to control for 'selection effects'. This is a variant of the correlation problem so beloved in statistical textbooks. Variable X may be highly correlated with 'dependent' variable Y, but this does not mean that X causes Y; rather both may be caused by an unacknowledged variable A. In this case becoming a young mother may not cause the poor outcomes—in terms of education, employment and income—experienced by many teenage mothers; rather both young motherhood, and poor outcomes, may be caused by pre-pregnancy social disadvantage. In this sense social disadvantage may 'select' particular young women, and men, to become teenage parents, and this disadvantage will continue post-pregnancy. Teenage parenting may therefore be a part of social disadvantage, rather than its cause. But if statistical studies do not control for these selection effects, then they will not be able to recognise this.

In fact there has been a tradition of statistical studies which do try to take account of these selection effects. Some researchers devised 'natural experiments' where selection effects would be better controlled, such as comparisons between cousins whose mothers were sisters, between sisters, or between twin sisters (only one of whom was a teenage mother), and between teenage mothers and other women who had conceived as a teenager but miscarried (who presumably would have gone on to become mothers). This type of research began in the USA, and found that the social outcome effects of mother's age at birth were very small, or as [economics professor] Saul Hoffman put it in his systematic review of the US research 'often essentially zero'. Indeed, by their mid/late twenties teenage mothers in the USA did better than miscarrying teenagers with regard to employment and income and this meant, ironically, that government spending would have increased if they had not become young mothers. . . .

Young Parents' Values and Experiences

What about the mothers and fathers themselves? A tradition of small-scale qualitative research focuses on their actual understandings and experiences of becoming a parent. In this way qualitative research can help explain just why the statistical studies find that age of pregnancy has little effect on social outcomes, and may actually make things better. While [researchers] Hilary Graham and Elizabeth McDermott see quantitative and qualitative research as contradictory (the former seeing teenage motherhood as a route to social exclusion, the latter as an act of social inclusion), this contradiction perhaps relates more to the way these results have been framed, interpreted and used within opposing discourses, rather than to the findings themselves. Instead, we can profitably see quantitative and qualitative studies as complementary in providing, on the one hand, extensive evidence about overall social patterns and, on the other, intensive evidence on the social processes that create these patterns.

What these qualitative studies find is that many mothers express positive attitudes to motherhood, and describe how motherhood has made them feel stronger, more competent, more connected to family and society, and more responsible.

Resilience in the face of constraints and stigma, based on a belief in the moral worth of being a mother, is one overriding theme. For some, this has given the impetus to change direction, or build on existing resources, so as to take up education, training and employment. There has been less research on young fathers, but what there has been tends to contradict the 'feckless' assumption. Like teenage mothers, most of the fathers are already socially disadvantaged, and it does not appear that fathering will in itself make this any worse. But, also like teen mothers, most express positive feelings about the child and want to be good fathers. Most contributed maintenance in some way, and many were actively involved in child care (this varies by age, with the youngest least likely to be involved.) And, like teenage mothers, there is some evidence that successful fathering could be a positive turning point in young men's lives. . . . Again, like teen mothers, young fathers may be less of a social threat, more of a social possibility.

That teenage motherhood has a positive side is an enduring finding over time in this research tradition. Nearly two decades ago, the study by Ann Phoenix of teenage mothers in London, in the mid-1980s, found that most of the mothers and their children were faring well. Most (and their male partners) had already done badly in the educational and employment systems, and it did not seem that early motherhood had caused this, or that deferring motherhood would have made much difference. Rather, if anything, motherhood was something of a turning point which 'spurred some women on' into education and employment. Contributions to this edited collection testify that, two decades later, this more positive picture remains pertinent. . . .

This positive theme is replicated in other national contexts. [Nursing professor] Lee SmithBattle's research in the USA is paradigmatic. She followed a small, diverse group of teenage mothers over 8 years, finding that many described mothering as a powerful catalyst for becoming more mature, and for redirecting their lives in positive ways. Mothering often 'anchors the self, fosters a sense of purpose and meaning, reweaves connections, and provides a new sense of future'. Indeed, two of the themes identified in a meta-synthesis of US qualitative studies of teenage mothers undertaken during the 1990s are 'motherhood as positively transforming' and 'baby as stabilising influence'. . . .

Rarely a Catastrophe

The evidence substantiated . . . shows that teenage childbirth does not often result from ignorance or low expectations, it is rarely a catastrophe for young women, and that teenage parenting does not particularly cause poor outcomes for mothers and their children. Expectations of motherhood can be high and parenting can be a positive experience for many young men and women. Furthermore, becoming a teenage parent can make good sense in the particular life worlds inhabited by some groups of young women and men. Policies about teenage parenting, however, assume the opposite. Unfortunately, this also means that policy will be misdirected in its aims, use inappropriate instruments, and may be unhelpful to many teenage parents.

VIEWPOINT 7

> *"Today, the rise of cohabiting households with children is the largest unrecognized threat to the quality and stability of children's family lives."*

Cohabitation Is Harmful to Parenting

Institute for American Values

In the following viewpoint, the Institute for American Values (IAV) argues that cohabitation—in which unmarried adults live together—is detrimental to parenting. The IAV highlights five negative themes found in cohabiting households: the decreased likelihood of children to thrive in such arrangements, exposure of children to family instability, increased family instability in American life, rise of "complex households" composed of partially related and unrelated members, and disproportionate rates and effects of cohabitation on poor communities. In summary, the institute claims that intact marriages are the "gold standard" for parenting. Founded in 1987, the IAV is a nonprofit, nonpartisan organization for the study and advocacy of American values.

"Executive Summary," *Why Marriage Matters: Thirty Conclusions from the Social Sciences*, Institute for American Values, 2011, pp. 1–6.

As you read, consider the following questions:

1. What statistics does the IAV provide for the growing rates of cohabitating households in the United States?
2. As described by the IAV, what are children in complex households more likely to report?
3. Why are not all marriages equal, in the IAV's view?

In the latter half of the twentieth century, divorce posed the biggest threat to marriage in the United States. Clinical, academic, and popular accounts addressing recent family change—from Judith [S.] Wallerstein's landmark book, *The Unexpected Legacy of Divorce*; to Sara McLanahan and Gary Sandefur's award-winning book, *Growing Up with a Single Parent*; to Barbara Dafoe Whitehead's attention-getting *Atlantic* article, "Dan Quayle Was Right"—focused largely on the impact that divorce had upon children, and rightly so. In the wake of the divorce revolution of the 1970s, divorce was the event most likely to undercut the quality and stability of children's family lives in the second half of the twentieth century.

No more. In fact, as divorce rates have come down since peaking in the early 1980s, children who are now born to married couples are actually more likely to grow up with both of their parents than were children born at the height of the divorce revolution. In fact, the divorce rate for married couples with children has fallen almost to pre–divorce revolution levels, with 23 percent of couples who married in the early 1960s divorcing before their first child turned ten, compared to slightly more than 23 percent for couples who married in the mid-1990s.

Today, the rise of cohabiting households with children is the largest unrecognized threat to the quality and stability of children's family lives. In fact, because of the growing prevalence of cohabitation, which has risen fourteen-fold since

1970, today's children are much more likely to spend time in a cohabiting household than they are to see their parents divorce.

Now, approximately 24 percent of the nation's children are born to cohabiting couples, which means that more children are currently born to cohabiting couples than to single mothers. Another 20 percent or so of children spend time in a cohabiting household with an unrelated adult at some point later in their childhood, often after their parents' marriage breaks down. This means that more than four in ten children are exposed to a cohabiting relationship. Thus, one reason that the institution of marriage has less of a hold over Americans than it has had for most our history is that cohabitation has emerged as a powerful alternative to and competitor with marriage. . . .

Five New Themes

1. Children are less likely to thrive in cohabiting households, compared to intact, married families. On many social, educational, and psychological outcomes, children in cohabiting households do significantly worse than children in intact, married families, and about as poorly as children living in single-parent families. And when it comes to abuse, recent federal data indicate that children in cohabiting households are markedly more likely to be physically, sexually, and emotionally abused than children in both intact, married families and single-parent families. Only in the economic domain do children in cohabiting households fare consistently better than children in single-parent families.

2. Family instability is generally bad for children. In recent years, family scholars have turned their attention to the impact that transitions into and out of marriage, cohabitation, and single parenthood have upon children. . . . Such transitions, especially multiple transitions, are linked to higher reports of school failure, behavioral problems, drug use, and loneliness, among other outcomes. So, it is not just family structure and family process that matter for children; family stability matters as well. And the research indicates that children who are born to married parents are the least likely to be exposed to family instability, and to the risks instability poses to the emotional, social, and educational welfare of children.

3. American family life is becoming increasingly unstable for children. Sociologist Andrew Cherlin has observed that Americans are stepping "on and off the carousel of intimate relationships" with increasing rapidity. This relational carousel spins particularly quickly for couples who are cohabiting, even cohabiting couples with children. For instance, cohabiting couples who have a child together are more than twice as likely to break up before their child turns twelve, compared to couples who are married to one another. Thus, one of the major reasons that children's lives are increasingly turbulent is that more and more children are being born into or raised in cohabiting households that are much more fragile than married families.

4. The growing instability of American family life also means that contemporary adults and children are more likely to live in what scholars call "complex households," where children and adults are living with people who are half siblings, stepsiblings, stepparents, stepchildren, or unrelated to them by birth or marriage. Research on these complex households is still embryonic, but the initial findings are not encouraging. For instance, one indicator of this growing complexity is multiple-partner fertility, where parents have children with more than one romantic partner. Children who come from these relationships are more likely to report poor relationships with their parents, to have behavioral and health problems, and to fail in school, even after controlling for factors such as education, income, and race. Thus, for both adults and children, life typically becomes not only more complex, but also more difficult, when parents fail to get or stay married.

Children in Cohabiting Homes and Poverty

Compared to children with married parents, 3 and 4 times as many children in cohabiting homes live in poverty depending upon the overall national economic conditions. In 2002, the poverty rate for all children in married-couple families was 8.2 percent, but for children in single-parent families the poverty rate was 4 times higher at 35.2 percent. Thus, poverty is one of the harshest results of the breakdown in traditional marriage and family, with women and children bearing the consequences most severely. Children living with cohabiters are more likely to be poor; less likely to have regular, nutritious meals; are read to infrequently; and exhibit more behavioral problems than children living with married parents.

Janice Shaw Crouse, Children at Risk: The Precarious State of Children's Well-Being in America. *New Brunswick, NJ: Transaction Publishers, 2010.*

5. *The nation's retreat from marriage has hit poor and working-class communities with particular force.* Recent increases in cohabitation, nonmarital childbearing, family instability, and family complexity have not been equally distributed in the United States; these trends, which first rose in poor communities in the 1970s and 1980s, are now moving rapidly into working-class and lower-middle-class communities. But marriage appears to be strengthening in more educated and affluent communities. As a consequence, since the early 1980s, children from college-educated homes have seen their family lives stabilize, whereas children from less educated homes have seen their family lives become increasingly unstable. More

generally, the stratified character of family trends means that the United States is "devolving into a separate-and-unequal family regime, where the highly educated and the affluent enjoy strong and stable [families] and everyone else is consigned to increasingly unstable, unhappy, and unworkable ones."

We acknowledge that social science is better equipped to document whether certain facts *are* true than to say *why* they are true. We can assert more definitively that marriage is associated with powerful social goods than that marriage is the sole or main cause of these goods.

A Word About Selection Effects

Good research seeks to tease out "selection effects," or the preexisting differences between individuals who marry, cohabit, or divorce. Does divorce cause poverty, for example, or is it simply that poor people are more likely to divorce? Scholars attempt to distinguish between causal relationships and mere correlations in a variety of ways. The studies cited here are for the most part based on large, nationally representative samples that control for race, education, income, and other confounding factors. In many, but not all cases, social scientists used longitudinal data to track individuals as they marry, divorce, or stay single, increasing our confidence that marriage itself matters. Where the evidence appears overwhelming that marriage *causes* increases in well-being, we say so. Where marriage probably does so but the causal pathways are not as well understood, we are more cautious.

We recognize that, absent random assignment to marriage, divorce, or single parenting, social scientists must always acknowledge the possibility that other factors are influencing outcomes. Reasonable scholars may and do disagree on the existence and extent of such selection effects and the extent to which marriage is causally related to the better social outcomes reported here.

Yet, scholarship is getting better in addressing selection effects. For instance, in this [viewpoint] we summarize three divorce studies that follow identical and nonidentical adult twins in Australia and Virginia to see how much of the effects of divorce on children are genetic and how much seem to be a consequence of divorce itself. Methodological innovations like these, as well as analyses using econometric models, afford us greater confidence that family structure exercises a causal influence for some outcomes.

Departures from the norm of intact marriage do not necessarily harm most of those who are exposed to them. While cohabitation is associated with increased risks of psychological and social problems for children, this does not mean that every child who is exposed to cohabitation is damaged. For example, one nationally representative study of six- to eleven-year-olds found that only 16 percent of children in cohabiting families experienced serious emotional problems. Still, this rate was much higher than the rate for children in families headed by married biological or adoptive parents, which was 4 percent.

While marriage is a social good, not all marriages are equal. Research does not generally support the idea that remarriage is better for children than living with a single mother. Marriages that are unhappy do not have the same benefits as the average marriage. Divorce or separation provides an important escape hatch for children and adults in violent or high-conflict marriages. Families, communities, and policy makers interested in distributing the benefits of marriage more equally must do more than merely discourage legal divorce.

But we believe good social science, despite its limitations, is a better guide to social policy than uninformed opinion or prejudice. This [viewpoint] represents our best judgment of what current social science evidence reveals about marriage in our social system.

Our Fundamental Conclusions

1. *The intact, biological, married family remains the gold standard for family life in the United States*, insofar as children are most likely to thrive—economically, socially, and psychologically—in this family form.

2. *Marriage is an important public good*, associated with a range of economic, health, educational, and safety benefits that help local, state, and federal governments serve the common good.

3. *The benefits of marriage extend to poor, working-class, and minority communities*, despite the fact that marriage has weakened in these communities in the last four decades.

Family structure and processes are only one factor contributing to child and social well-being. Our discussion here is not meant to minimize the importance of other factors, such as poverty, child support, unemployment, teenage childbearing, neighborhood safety, or the quality of education for both parents and children. Marriage is not a panacea for all social ills. For instance, when it comes to child well-being, research suggests that family structure is a better predictor of children's psychological and social welfare, whereas poverty is a better predictor of educational attainment.

But whether we succeed or fail in building a healthy marriage culture is clearly a matter of legitimate public concern and an issue of paramount importance if we wish to reverse the marginalization of the most vulnerable members of our society: the working class, the poor, minorities, and children.

VIEWPOINT

"Just as so many of us have learned to make marriages work without the support of a religious community, we can probably manage partnerships without a wedding."

Cohabitation May Not Be Harmful to Parenting

Lauren Sandler

Cohabitation is when an unwed couple forms a household. In the following viewpoint, Lauren Sandler suggests that cohabitation is perceived as harmful to parenting because it is not yet a social norm. While concerned with a study that claims to expose the disadvantages and setbacks experienced by children in these homes, Sandler proposes that these conclusions are related to perceptions and stereotypes of unmarried parents and other non-normative family structures. Indeed, the author asserts that the definitions of partnership and parenting do not have to revert to the traditional model of marriage. Sandler is a journalist living in New York.

Lauren Sandler, "Cohabitation Is Only a Problem Because It's Not Normal Yet," *Slate*, August 17, 2011.

As you read, consider the following questions:

1. How do families and children differ in Sweden, as told by Sandler?
2. Why will kids in cohabiting households continue to feel distress, in Sandler's view?
3. What does Sandler conclude about society's progress with re-forming notions of partnerships?

Yesterday [August 16, 2011], the National Marriage Project released a major report stating that cohabitation is the biggest threat to American children, eclipsing divorce and overshadowing single motherhood. While the study's authors, led by the University of Virginia's Brad Wilcox, admit that this is more of an issue for black and low-income families (which are more likely to have unmarried parents), the authors say that all kids "exposed to cohabitation"—as if it were a disease, or a fatal contaminant—have more emotional problems, less involved and less affectionate fathers, a greater risk of school failure, a higher risk of infant mortality, and worse physical health than kids with married parents. That's despite economics, class, or race.

Cohabitation Is Not Equal to Marriage

"Cohabitation is not a functional equivalent of marriage," the study claims. And as Wilcox said at an event last night at the Institute for American Values, where he discussed the study, "cohabitation and kids don't mix."

In an interview this morning, I asked Wilcox how my kid—the daughter of married parents—will fare compared to the children of my unmarried friends. He told me that my daughter will always know that her parents made a commitment to each other, and transversely, to her, and that society lauds that commitment. Her friends with cohabitating parents will never have that stability, the assurance of that socially accepted bond.

Philosophically, I want to disagree with him. But doesn't he also have a point? My 3-year-old is already fascinated by who is married and who isn't and what it means. I must have been, too, to some extent—I was a reluctant bride, but I've worn a wedding ring for almost a decade. Sure, my partner and I co-parent, my work takes equal precedence, and our partnership has about as much gender parity as I can imagine. But I still bought the dress and got hitched. People say getting married requires strength, but I think it may have been the wimpiest thing I've ever done. Perhaps I'm one of the many people who, as University of Pennsylvania professor Amy Wax put it at last night's event, could be accused of "thinking the '60s, but living the '50s."

And despite my intellectual resistance to the data in the new report, when I read through the data, I feel anxiety. The data on cohabitating parents depict a world no one would want for her child: a world where fathers don't hug, kids don't graduate, already sensitive adolescent psyches are further strained, and it's harder to negotiate one's own safety and mores. The study reminds us that children fare worse in complex arrangements—cohabitation included—in which roles feel undefined and accountability may be weak.

Marriage Is Still Worshipped

I'm currently researching a book on only children and have come across a great deal of analysis on how children growing up in non-normative family structures are made to feel like outsiders. I can't help but wonder if the psychological stress of being raised by cohabiting parents is akin to the experience of being an (oft-stereotyped) only child, at least in the upper economic brackets. In Sweden, where it's become normal to parent without a marriage certificate, kids with unmarried parents don't feel this way. But here, as long as marriage is worshipped, supported by friends and family and strangers and the state, as long as kids who are inside a married family know that they are what's normal and that those other kids aren't, there will be distress. Nobody wants to feel like his or her family is an experiment. Or that other people get to be supported by stability they are lacking.

This doesn't mean that in re-forming our notion of partnership we have to revert to the marriages of the '50s, as was implied in much of last night's discussion (in front of an audience that applauded when "the edu-crats" were lambasted for teaching sex ed). Instead, we need to re-norm healthy partnerships. Just as so many of us have learned to make marriages work without the support of a religious community, we can probably manage partnerships without a wedding. But the study is clear about one thing, which I have to square emotionally, and you might too: We're not there yet, and my marriage, strong and seemingly progressive as it is, may not be helping to re-norm a damn thing.

Periodical and Internet Sources Bibliography

The following articles have been selected to supplement the diverse views presented in this chapter.

Deborah Taj Anapol	"Polyamory and Children," *Love Without Limits* (blog), *Psychology Today*, March 25, 2011.
Lisa Belkin	"What's Good for the Kids," *New York Times*, November 5, 2009.
Ann Brenoff	"'Too Old to Adopt'? Not the Case for These Parents," *Huffington Post*, July 3, 2012.
Marjorie Campbell	"Listening to the Children of Gay Parents," *Crisis Magazine*, July 25, 2008.
Camilla Chafer	"'I'm Glad I Was a Teenage Mother,'" *Independent* (UK), December 8, 2009.
Charles C.W. Cooke	"Is Gay Parenting Bad for the Kids?," *National Review Online*, June 10, 2012.
Ann Coulter	"Secondhand Children," Townhall.com, February 4, 2009.
Mike Males	"The Real Mistake in 'Teen Pregnancy,'" *Los Angeles Times*, July 13, 2008.
Lisa Rogers	"In Praise of Single Mothers: Why I'm Glad I Was Raised by a Single Mom," MyDaily.com, February 24, 2011.
Katie Roiphe	"Single Moms Are Crazy!," *Slate*, October 5, 2011.
Shirley S. Wang	"This Is Your Brain Without Dad," *Wall Street Journal*, October 27, 2009.

CHAPTER 3

Are Parents Liable for Their Children's Actions?

Chapter Preface

In 2011 the National Center for Education Statistics found that 28 percent of students between the ages of twelve and eighteen—or more than seven million—reported that they had been bullied on campus during the 2008–2009 school year. Among these students, 36.3 percent reported that a teacher or other adult at school was notified about the bullying. In addition, 6 percent reported that they were victims of cyberbullying, which often takes place on computers and mobile devices off campus.

Some argue that parents must take responsibility if their child bullies or harasses others. Karen Siris, a bullying expert and principal at Oceanside School District in New York State, insists that such conduct is shaped by how kids are raised and treated. "Research about bullying tells us that children with bullying behaviors come from a home where there are rejecting behaviors and a lack of warmth; where the bully's primary caretaker is often permissive and allows aggressive behavior toward peers, siblings, and adults; and where a bully is often subjected to physical punishment and exposed to violent outbursts by his or her caretaker," she asserts in a bulletin published by the School Administrators Association of New York State. "It is particularly important for schools to speak to the parents of children with bullying behaviors about these issues so that they can provide warm and supportive environments for their children," Siris advises.

However, others point out that there are no easy answers for parents to prevent bullying. Fran Bell Baruch, a writer based in Los Angeles, California, said that talking to her son and meeting with school faculty and experts did not end his bad behavior. "I think it's too easy sometimes to blame the parents for everything when every situation is different. It's a scary subject, bullying," Baruch says in an interview on *The*

Takeaway, a radio news program. Moreover, family columnist Lisa Belkin suggests that parents "cannot know everything about their children" and are not "mind readers." She recommends, however, that parents pay attention when a child has a tendency to gossip or look down on others. In the following chapter, the authors investigate both the responsibilities and liabilities of being a parent.

Viewpoint 1

"Today, most states have laws relating to parental liability in various applications."

Parents May Be Liable for Their Children's Actions

FindLaw

In the following viewpoint, FindLaw discusses when parents are liable for the actions of their children—starting between the ages of eight and ten—as well as the types of liabilities. FindLaw explains that each state differs in its laws for the parental civil liability for minors' offenses—such as the defacement or destruction of property—through the legal concept of vicarious liability. Parental criminal liability is recognized when children gain access to firearms, commit Internet crimes, and—depending on state law—engage in acts as delinquent youths, FindLaw adds. Finally, it advises that parents can be held liable when leaving a child alone at home or without adult supervision. FindLaw is a website that provides free legal information and online marketing for law firms.

As you read, consider the following questions:

1. According to FindLaw, what are the characteristics of civil and criminal cases?
2. What is negligent supervision, as stated by FindLaw?
3. What provision do some states have for criminal liability of custodial adults or parents when children possess firearms, as told by FindLaw?

Parental liability is the term used to refer to a parent's obligation to pay for damage caused by negligent, intentional, or criminal acts committed by the parent's child. Parental liability usually ends when the child reaches the age of majority and does not begin until the child reaches an age of between eight and ten. Today, most states have laws relating to parental liability in various applications. Children's offenses can be civil and/or criminal in nature. Civil cases are lawsuits for money damages. The government brings criminal cases for violations of criminal law. Many acts can trigger both civil and criminal legal repercussions.

Civil Parental Liability

In most states, parents are responsible for all malicious or willful property damage done by their children. Laws vary from state to state regarding the monetary limits on damages that can be collected, the age limit of the child, and the inclusion of personal injury in the tort claim. Hawaii's parental liability law remains one of the most broadly applied in that it does not limit the financial bounds of recovery, and imposes liability for both negligent and intentional torts [wrongful acts] by underage persons.

Criminal Parental Liability

Laws making parents criminally responsible for the delinquent acts of their children followed civil liability statutes. In 1903, Colorado became the first state to establish the crime of "contributing to the delinquency of a minor."

Minors

A minor is a person under the age of majority. The age of majority is the age at which a minor, in the eyes of the law, becomes an adult. This age is 18 in most states. In a few other states, the age of majority is 19 or 21. A minor is considered to be a resident of the same state as the minor's custodial parent or guardian.

Insurance Coverage

Since homeowners insurance includes both property and liability coverage, wrongful acts of children or negligent supervision claims may be covered even if the act took place away from a policyholder's residence. Homeowners policies typically cover legal liability in the event that anyone suffers an injury while on the insured property, even if the injury was committed by another household member or the result of negligence on the part of the policyholder.

Parental Civil Liability

Each state has its own law regarding parents' civil (noncriminal) liability for the acts of their children. Parents are responsible for their children's harmful actions much the same way that employers are responsible for the harmful actions of their employees. This legal concept is known a vicarious liability. The parent is vicariously liable, despite not being directly responsible for the injury. A number of states hold parents financially responsible for damages caused by their children. Some of these states, however, place limits on the amount of liability. Parental civil liability laws vary from state to state, but many cover such acts as:

- Vandalism to government or school property;
- Defacement or destruction of the national and state flags, cemetery headstones, public monuments/historical markers; and

- Property destroyed in hate crimes, based on race or religion, such as ransacking a synagogue.

Personal injury in connection with any of these acts may also be included in parental civil liability laws.

Negligent Supervision

A parent is liable for a child's negligent acts if the parent knows or has reason to know that it is necessary to control the child and the parent fails to take reasonable actions to do so. This legal theory is known as negligent supervision. Liability for negligent supervision is not limited to parents. Grandparents, guardians, and others with custody and control of a child may also be liable under these circumstances. There is usually no dollar limit on this type of liability. An umbrella or homeowners insurance policy may offer the adult some protection in a lawsuit.

The "Family Car" Doctrine

The "family car" doctrine holds the owner of a family car legally responsible for any damage caused by a family member when driving, if the owner knew of—and consented to—the family member's use of the car. This doctrine is applied by about half of the states. Thus, even if a parent does not have a minor household member listed on the auto insurance policy, under the family car doctrine the adult remains liable. Most insurance policies have special provisions for members of the household under eighteen. Typically, minor drivers must be included on the policy. The car owner would not be able to invoke the uninsured motorist provision for a minor child driver residing in the insured's household and driving the insured's vehicle.

Parental Criminal Liability

Firearm Access Laws

Some states have laws which hold parents criminally liable when children gain access to firearms. At least nine states hold adults criminally responsible for storing a loaded firearm in

The General Rule Regarding Parental Liability

The general rule regarding parental liability is that the mere relationship between parent and child does not impose any legal liability on the parent for the bad acts or carelessness of the child. Rather, parents are held liable only when the child is acting as an agent of the parent or when some carelessness of the parent made the bad act possible. Some examples regarding parental liability as an agent include harm resulting from a car accident caused by the negligence of a child when the child was running an errand for a parent, or when a parent encourages a child to physically attack another person. Parents also can be held liable when their own negligence contributes to a child causing injury to another. For instance, if a parent serves a child alcohol and then permits the child to drive a car, the parent may be liable for damages. Thus, for a parent to be found liable for the behavior of his or her child, the child must be acting on behalf of the parent or the parent must have made the harm possible through his or her own carelessness or negligence.

Robert M. Regoli, John D. Hewitt, and Matt DeLisi, Delinquency in Society. *Sudbury, MA: Jones & Bartlett Learning, 2009.*

such a way as to allow a minor to gain access. Some of these provisions include an enhanced penalty if the minor causes injury or death. Other state laws create exceptions for parental liability when the minor gains access to a weapon by unlawful entry into the home or place of storage, or if the firearm is used in self-defense. In addition, several states have provisions that create criminal liability when a custodial adult or parent is aware that his or her child possesses a firearm unlawfully and does not take it away. A number of jurisdictions have enacted laws making it a crime to leave a loaded firearm where it is accessible by children. Typically, these laws apply—and parents can be charged—only if the minor gains access to the gun. There are usually exceptions if the firearm is stored in a locked box and/or secured with a trigger lock. In most states, the penalty for unlawful access is a misdemeanor unless the minor injures someone else, in which case the parent can be charged with a felony.

Internet Access and Computer Hacking

Another parental criminal liability issue involves certain unlawful computer and Internet activities committed by minors. In 2003, the Recording Industry Association [of America] sued 261 persons for downloading protected music onto their personal computers and infringing copyrights. Among the defendants were several surprised parents who had no knowledge of their minor child's downloading activities. In *Thrifty-Tel[, Inc.] v. Bezenek* the California Court of Appeals upheld a verdict against the parents of juvenile computer hackers who accessed the phone company's network in order to make long distance calls without cost. And with the appearance of camera cell phones and computer video cameras in the early 2000s, the opportunity for minors to sell pornographic images of themselves or otherwise engage in illegal Internet activities has increased dramatically. In such matters, federal law may preempt state laws and provide a more uniform guidance for resolution. However, these examples point to the need for a more comprehensive approach to parental liability across state lines.

Delinquent Youth

Although some states impose criminal liability on parents of delinquent youth, many more have enacted less stringent types of parental responsibility laws. Kansas, Michigan, and Texas require parents to attend the hearings of children adjudicated delinquent or face contempt charges. Legislation in Alabama, Kansas, Kentucky, and West Virginia requires parents to pay the court costs associated with these proceedings. Other states impose financial responsibility on parents for the costs incurred by the state when youth are processed through the juvenile justice system. Florida, Idaho, Indiana, North Carolina, and Virginia require parents to reimburse the state for the costs associated with the care, support, detention, or treatment of their children while under the supervision of state agencies. Idaho, Maryland, Missouri, and Oklahoma require parents to undertake restitution payments.

When Can a Child Be Left Home Alone?

The 1990 movie *Home Alone* may have poked fun at what could happen when an eight-year-old boy is accidentally left home alone, yet in reality it is not uncommon for thousands of American children to be left home alone on any given day. Children who are left home alone—sometimes known as "latchkey kids"—are often left without adult supervision for reasons beyond a parent's control and, in some unfortunate situations, out of neglect or child abuse.

For anyone considering whether it is alright to leave a child at home alone, there are important safety and legal guidelines to consider before leaving any child unsupervised for any extended period of time.

Laws for Leaving a Child Home Alone

Only a couple of states have laws that specify the age when a child can be left home alone, including Maryland (age 8) and Illinois (age 14). However, most states have guidelines with the Department of Health and Human Services or other child protective agencies that test a child's ability to be left home alone. Factors may include the child's age and maturity, the overall safety of the surrounding area/circumstances, and arrangements made to secure the child's safety.

Below are general guidelines to follow when considering the age range for leaving a child home alone.

7 & under—Should not be left alone for any period of time. This may include leaving children unattended in cars, playgrounds, and backyards. The determining consideration would be the dangers in the environment and the ability of the caretaker to intervene.

8 to 10 years—Should not be left alone for more than 1½ hours and only during daylight and early evening hours.

11 to 12 years—May be left alone for up to 3 hours but not late at night or in circumstances requiring inappropriate responsibility.

13 to 15 years—May be left unsupervised, but not overnight.

16 to 17 years—May be left unsupervised (in some cases, for up to two consecutive overnight periods).

VIEWPOINT

"One of the foundations of parental responsibility laws seems to be the negative relationship between parental monitoring and juvenile delinquency."

Parental Liability Laws Attempt to Promote Parental Monitoring

Eve M. Brank and Jodi Lane

In the following viewpoint, Eve M. Brank and Jodi Lane suggest that a main purpose of parental liability laws is to encourage parents to monitor their children. Research demonstrates that youths who engage in illegal behavior are more likely to have parents who are not directly involved in their lives or poor parent-child relationships, the authors observe. In addition, parental liability laws draw from the deterrence theory, wherein punishment for the parents is thought to reduce juvenile delinquency, Brank and Lane claim. Brank is an assistant professor of psychology at the University of Nebraska-Lincoln. Lane is an associate professor of criminology and law at the University of Florida.

Eve M. Brank and Jodi Lane, "Punishing My Parents: Juveniles' Perspectives on Parental Responsibility," *Criminal Justice Policy Review (CJPR)*, vol. 19, no. 3, September 2008, pp. 333–336. Reproduced with permission of SAGE PUBLICATIONS INC. via Copyright Clearance Center.

As you read, consider the following questions:

1. As stated by the authors, what are some opinions of scholars who are critical of parental liability laws?
2. What other parental behavior is related to a decrease in delinquency, as claimed by the authors?
3. What do the authors speculate about the connection between youths' perceptions of negative consequences for parents and deterrence?

In a little more than a hundred years, the juvenile justice system has largely transformed from the original parens patriae [the state or government as parent] notions into a system based on blame, responsibility, and accountability. In the same states where legislators once called the wayward youth to be brought back into the folds of society, they now call for determinate sentencing and enhanced penalties when youth break the law. Clearly, the law places legal accountability on juveniles, but the law has also placed increasingly more accountability on the parents of those children.

Based on state legislation and city council attention to the topic of parental responsibility laws, it is clear that lawmakers support accountability for parents whose children commit delinquent acts. The public's support of this accountability appears to be present, but possibly less intense than anecdotal media stories portray. . . .

Parental Responsibility Laws

Although not a new concept, holding parents accountable for the crimes their children commit has gained attention in recent years as the media and legislators are focusing more attention on parental responsibility laws. These laws generally come in three different forms at the state level: civil liability, contributing to the delinquency of a minor, and parental involvement. The third type is the newest and most controversial. For example, in Florida, the site of the current research, parents can be required to attend parenting classes or counseling when it is deemed necessary for the rehabilitation of the child or to aid the parents in their abilities to raise the child. Among other things, the court has the discretion to order the parents to perform community service or make restitution if the parents did not make a "diligent and good faith effort" to prevent the delinquency. Currently, no cases have addressed this statutory terminology that makes it difficult to know exactly what parental actions the courts will consider as diligent and in good faith. City ordinances reflecting this third type of law require parents to participate in community service or pay fines when their children break laws such as city curfews. Although none of these forms of law is particularly new, they often gain public attention after a major youth crime, like a school shooting or gang violence. Despite the media attention after a major crime, some evidence suggests that the laws are used rather infrequently.

Legal scholars have mixed reactions to parental responsibility issues with many arguing that the laws are not legitimate exercises of the juvenile court power. Some scholars are especially critical and see parental responsibility laws as nothing more than symbolic politics and argue that they will only continue to perpetrate the disadvantage of single and minority mothers. Others contend that these notions are appropriate and based on the well-supported concept of parental monitoring.

Parental Monitoring

One of the foundations of parental responsibility laws seems to be the negative relationship between parental monitoring and juvenile delinquency. Research has repeatedly demonstrated that the children who participate in illegal behavior are more likely to come from homes where the parents are not actively involved in the juveniles' lives or have poor parent-child relationships. Less parent supervision is also related to a greater likelihood of having delinquent friends.

In addition to parental monitoring, open communication between juveniles and their parents is related to a decrease in delinquency. Other parental behaviors such as hostility toward or rejection of their children are related to increased rates of delinquency. Juveniles who are exposed to violence in their homes are also more likely to report delinquent behaviors. Clearly, research has demonstrated a connection between parental behaviors and a juvenile's delinquency. The question remains whether appropriate parental behaviors can be enforced through parental responsibility legislation.

Parental Responsibility and Criminological Theory

The legal focus on parental monitoring fits nicely within some tenets of criminological theory as well. [Michael R.] Gottfredson and [Travis] Hirschi's *A General Theory of Crime* argues that parents are the major problem that produces low self-control, the key factor in criminality according to the theory. These theorists argue that for children to be taught self-control, "the person who cares for the child will watch his behavior, see him doing things he should not do, and correct him." From this perspective, parents might fail to care for the child at all, fail to monitor the child's behavior, fail to notice that behaviors are wrong, or fail to punish the child when problematic behaviors arise. Any of these failures could lead to low self-control in the child and possibly delinquency. In trying to improve parental monitoring and involvement among youths in the juvenile justice system, the laws are essentially attempting to force good parenting or at least prevent major failures in these key areas.

These laws also seem to be based on the tenets of deterrence theory, or the idea that the threat of punishing the parents will prevent youths from committing crimes (either indirectly through increased parental control or directly by affecting the juvenile's decision about whether or not to commit delinquency). Some studies on deterrence, but not all, have found that a person's perception of a higher risk of getting caught and punished is associated with less self-reported offending or expectations of offending. We know of no other studies examining the connection between youths' perceptions of negative consequences for others, such as parents, and individual deterrence effects. It is at least theoretically possible however, that the more attached youths are to their parents, the more they would worry about the effects of their own behavior on them. This might be especially true if the families face financial hardship, regularly struggling to "make ends meet," and the threatened punishment involves financial penalties for parents, as it does in Florida. In contrast, youths who are in trouble may have fewer bonds to their parents and therefore may be less likely to be deterred by legal threats of punishment.

Public Opinion on Juvenile Crime and Parental Responsibility Laws

The public has taken a fairly punitive stance toward juvenile offenders even in light of the recent reductions in juvenile crime. The best-interest standard originally envisioned for the juvenile justice system has given way to a system that holds juveniles accountable for their actions in a very similar way to [how] the criminal justice system holds adults accountable for their crimes and readily transfers juveniles into the adult criminal justice system. The one caveat to the juvenile accountability model is the parental responsibility laws that remove some of the responsibility away from the juveniles and place it on the parents.

Because parental responsibility laws seem to run counter to the general juvenile accountability notions, early research in the area of parental responsibility mainly focused on public opinion concerning these laws. National polls indicated that many adults saw the parents as blameworthy for the Columbine school shootings [a high school shooting in Colorado in 1999], although they also blamed television, movies, music, and social pressures. When asked more generally about parents' responsibility, nearly 70% of the respondents to a national Gallup telephone poll indicated that the parents, in addition to the juvenile, were responsible when a teenager commits a crime. Similarly, almost half of the 2,000 adults surveyed by Public Agenda Online thought that the difficulties facing kids today were the result of irresponsible parents. Some research has examined the public support on a deeper level by comparing global versus specific attitudes. Similar to other global and specific research that demonstrates attitude inconsistency, people were more supportive of parental responsibility notions when they were asked generally rather than when asked about a case description of a specific juvenile offender and his parents.

Viewpoint 

> *"In each case, it's up to the kids—not the parents—to pay the bill."*

Some Parental Financial Liability Laws Are Not Effective

Steve Mayes

Steve Mayes is a reporter for the Oregonian, *a daily newspaper based in Portland, Oregon. In the following viewpoint, Mayes contends that laws for parental financial liability for children's offenses rarely provide compensation for the victims. He cites numerous Oregon cases in which minors were ruled responsible for restitution even though they have limited or no resources to pay. Parents may be sued for the crimes of their kids, Mayes says, but the financial liability of adults is capped. Furthermore, while laws and ordinances to hold parents accountable are periodically adopted, they are rarely used or fully enforced, he claims.*

As you read, consider the following questions:

1. What example of an alternative does Mayes provide of allowing youths to pay their victims?

Steve Mayes, "In Oregon, Parental Responsibility Rarely Requires Compensating Victims of Their Children's Crimes," *The Oregonian*, December 3, 2011.

2. How does Mayes characterize America's interest in parental liability?
3. What statement does Leslie Harris give in the viewpoint about holding parents accountable?

A 14-year-old Sandy [Oregon] boy toppled trees and power poles onto a dark Oregon highway, injuring and endangering motorists. A 13-year-old Oregon City boy pointed a loaded shotgun at a neighbor boy, leaving him with permanent brain damage when the gun went off. A group of Happy Valley children trashed a vacant house they used as a party pad.

In each case, the children faced juvenile court judges who handed out penalties, a mix of detention, community service or restitution. And in each case, it's up to the kids—not the parents—to pay the bill.

In the brain-injury case, the judge ordered the boy's mother and father to take parenting classes and may hold the child, who pleaded guilty to assault responsible for paying the victim's family more than $100,000.

"Just once, I'd like to see a parent held accountable for the actions of their delinquent kid," said a reader commenting on OregonLive. "Parenting isn't difficult. It's just time-consuming. . . ."

In 1995, the Oregon legislature felt the same way and passed a law that makes failure to supervise a child a violation that could require a parent to pay up to $2,500 in restitution—but only after a second conviction. After the first violation, a judge can order defendants to complete a "parent effectiveness program." Parents also may avoid conviction if they can show they took "reasonable steps to control the conduct of the child."

It is a little-used statute.

Another Oregon law allows victims to sue the parents of children who cause harm to people or property. But parents face limited liability: There is a $7,500 cap, and it applies only to actual damages.

"It's very difficult for victims (of juvenile crimes) to be compensated for their losses," said Tom Cleary, a Multnomah County senior deputy district attorney who heads the juvenile unit.

It is the rare teenager who has the resources to pay restitution.

Sometimes there are alternatives. Multnomah County operates a community service program [that] allows youths to earn a little money that is then paid to victims.

"The system seems not to make available remedies that allow people to be made whole," said Clackamas County circuit judge Douglas V. Van Dyk, who has handled juvenile cases for nine years.

Parental Responsibility

America's interest in holding parents accountable for their children rises and falls. The fervor began in the early 1900s and last peaked in the mid-1990s.

Oregon once had a law making it illegal to contribute to the delinquency of a minor. The statute was found unconstitutional in 1969.

And so it went for 25 years.

Then cities across the country relit the torch.

Silverton passed a parental responsibility ordinance in 1994, focusing national attention on the movie-set perfect small town just outside Salem.

"It's a fad . . . an idea that's always lurking out there," said University of Oregon law professor Leslie Harris. "A politician can make some hay saying, 'I'm doing something about teenage crime and the breakdown of family values, and it's free. It doesn't cost anything."

So it was in Oregon, where lawmakers quickly climbed aboard, passing a similar law the following year. Like local ordinances, the state law targeted parents who failed to deal with small infractions—such as truancy and curfew violations—that serve as warning signs.

"I firmly believe this law will help us bring juvenile crime under control and get to their kids and parents early enough so that children do not get mired in a life of crime," said Gov. John Kitzhaber, then in his first term.

Soon, the glow dimmed.

Harris surveyed police and prosecutors across Oregon in 2001 to see whether the state law had impact.

Her conclusion then: "It's not used much." And it still isn't.

Towns that adopted ordinances, however, use them to varying degrees.

"It's used in situations where we've run out of options," said Baker City police chief Wyn Lohner.

The city uses both its own ordinance and state law to cite parents for infractions such as failing to control underage drinking at their kids' home parties, failing to send their children to school or failing to ensure that a child under house arrest stays home.

Canby passed an ordinance but "I don't think we've ever used it," said city attorney John Kelley.

Since January 2008, Silverton police issued parents 117 warnings and eight citations.

"It's a nice tool to have. It's fair. We're not out trying to hammer the parents. We're trying to educate and give them a chance to correct the problem," said Deputy Chief Jeff Fossholm. In three cases, families left town before their cases landed in court. "They're probably still going to be a problem . . . but they weren't going to be a problem in Silverton," he said.

Harris, the law professor, said holding parents accountable "plays to a very widely held intuitively obvious idea that parenting is important and if parents did a good job kids wouldn't mess up."

"We believe all those things . . . and there's truth in them," said Harris, "it's just when you start thinking about them in a more serious way you go, 'Hmm, it's a little more complicated than that.'"

VIEWPOINT 

"If teens don't learn to drink responsibly at home, some parents fear they will learn on their own, in a club or private party, where there are few restraints."

Dad, I Prefer the Shiraz

Melinda Beck

In the following viewpoint, Melinda Beck explains why some parents supervise their children's drinking at home. These parents believe that allowing teens to consume alcohol in moderation with family can deter binge drinking elsewhere, she states. However, the research on parental involvement in underage drinking is mixed, Beck notes. One survey indicates that teens who drank with their parents were less likely to binge or drink regularly, she says, but a study found that teen bingeing was higher in numerous European countries, where minimum drinking ages are lower or nonexistent. The author writes the weekly Health Journal column for the Wall Street Journal.

As you read, consider the following questions:

1. In Beck's opinion, what is the position of parents who oppose underage drinking at home?

2. Although the national minimum drinking age is twenty-one, what do some states allow, as described by the author?

3. What type of parenting does the author say is more effective at keeping children from abusing alcohol?

Parents teach their children how to swim, how to ride a bicycle and how to drive. Should they also teach their teenagers how to drink responsibly?

The volatile issue is seldom discussed at alcohol-awareness programs. But some parents do quietly allow their teens to have wine or beer at home occasionally, figuring that kids who drink in moderation with their family may be less likely to binge on their own.

Many other parents argue that underage drinking of any kind is dangerous and illegal, and that parents who allow it are sending an irresponsible message that could set teens up for alcohol abuse in later years.

U.S. government surveys have started tracking where and how teenagers obtain alcohol—and that at least some of the time, parents are the suppliers.

Nearly 6% of 12- to 14-year-olds—some 700,000 middle schoolers—drank alcohol in the past month. And nearly 45% of them got it free at home, including 16% who obtained it from a parent or guardian, according to a report released last month by the Substance Abuse and Mental Health Services Administration (SAMHSA). The survey doesn't report how much alcohol was involved or what the circumstances were.

"This report isn't designed to say, 'Bad parents!' It's designed to say, 'Here's an issue you should pay attention to,'" says Peter Delany, director of SAMHSA's Center for Behavioral Health Statistics and Quality. "When kids under age 15 start drinking and drinking heavily, they are about six times more likely to end up with alcohol problems."

Zits used with permission of the Zits Partnership, King Features Syndicate and the Cartoonist Group.

Still, some parents think it's inevitable that teenagers will experiment with alcohol and worry that a message of abstinence doesn't stand a chance against a barrage of social pressures and media messages glamorizing drinking. By the time they turn 21, 86% of American youths have used alcohol, according to the 2009 National Survey on Drug Use and Health, and 50% are binge drinking, defined as having five or more drinks in a single session for men, and four or more for women.

If teens don't learn to drink responsibly at home, some parents fear they will learn on their own, in a club or private party, where there are few restraints.

Stanton Peele, a psychologist and author of books on addiction, also questions whether any kind of drinking before age 15 carries the same six-fold risk of alcohol problems. "There's a giant difference between a kid who gets totally wasted on some purloined booze in the woods with his friends, and someone who has wine at dinner with their parents or as part of a religious ceremony," he says.

Although the minimum drinking age is 21 in all 50 states, 31 states allow parents, guardians or spouses to furnish alcohol to minors. In seven of the 31 states, that's permissible only in a private residence.

Research on parents' role in underage drinking has been limited. A survey of 6,245 U.S. teens, published in the *Journal of Adolescent Health* in 2004, found that adults play a very important role in teen drinking—but in different ways. Teens who attended a party where alcohol was supplied by a parent were twice as likely to have engaged in binge drinking and twice as likely to be regular drinkers. But teens who drank along with their parents were only one-third as likely to binge and half as likely to be regular drinkers.

Many teens grow up drinking wine with their parents as an accompaniment to meals in wine-producing countries like Italy and France, where there is no minimum legal drinking age. But research is mixed on whether such teens are more or less likely to be problem drinkers.

A World Health Organization report found that 1-in-10 drinking occasions by 15- and 16-year-olds in southern European countries resulted in intoxication, compared with almost half in the U.S.

But the 2003 European School Survey Project on Alcohol and Other Drugs found that the proportion of 15- to 16-year-olds who binge drink is higher in France and Italy than in the U.S. Bingeing is even more prevalent in Denmark, Ireland, the U.K. and other northern European countries where drinking is usually done in bars rather than at home with meals.

U.S. government agencies and scores of alcohol-awareness groups say that no amount of underage drinking is permissible, and that no matter where it comes from, teens who drink alcohol are at extra risk of being involved in motor-vehicle crashes, homicides, suicides and accidents of all kinds, as well as unplanned sex, unplanned pregnancies and sexually transmitted diseases.

"Underage drinking is not safe, and it's not the case that somehow the risk is removed because the parents provided it," says Michael Hilton, acting deputy director for epidemiology and prevention research at the National Institute on Alcohol Abuse and Alcoholism.

Research also suggests that alcohol can do long-term harm to developing brains. In the late teens and early 20s, the brain is developing its adult shape, pruning away unused connections and forming permanent pathways, particularly in areas involved in planning, decision making and impulse control.

Brain scans have shown that heavy drinking—20 drinks or more a month—in adolescents can create changes in the frontal cortex, the hippocampus and white matter, leading to decreased cognitive function, executive function, memory, attention and spatial skills, researchers at the University of California, San Diego wrote in the *Journal of Clinical EEG and Neuroscience* in 2009.

The researchers did not see such dramatic changes in adolescents who drank more moderately. But the report didn't determine a "safe" level of alcohol. Indeed, experts say more research is needed to understand what puts young people at risk for alcohol abuse in later years and what strategies are best to discourage it.

In the meantime, some parents remain stumped about what to say to their children about alcohol. Several studies have found that parents who are authoritative—communicating expectations with a give-and-take style with their children—are more effective at keeping them from alcohol abuse than those who are authoritarian, permissive or disengaged. What's often lost in the discussions is that many teens are not regular drinkers. In a national survey of 500,000 students starting college last summer, 70% of youths aged 12 to 20 haven't had a drink in the last month.

For his part, Dr. Delany says he's been very clear with his 14-year-old son. "I think that using alcohol and drugs is not healthy. It's not just a matter of cognitive decision making. His body is maturing."

He also suggests discussing upcoming situations with teenagers. "You can say, 'There may be a lot of people drinking.

Have you thought about how you're going to handle that?' Then really listen to their answers."

VIEWPOINT

"Parents who are hosting underage drinking parties are not helping their kids. They are breaking the law."

Parents May Be Liable for Allowing Children to Drink at Home

Lucinda Masterton

Lucinda Masterton is judge for the Fifth Division of the Fayette County Family Court in Kentucky. In the following viewpoint, she warns that parents who host underage drinking parties for their children at home may be liable for the potential consequences. Masterton says that most states hold adults criminally liable for serving alcohol to minors, known as social host liability, whether or not the homeowners know about the parties. Parents may also be civilly liable for the injury, deaths, or damage caused by the minors to whom they serve alcohol, she persists. Most importantly, the author argues, is the danger alcohol use poses to children, including violence, risky sexual behavior, and even death.

Lucinda Masterton, "Underage Drinking Parties Open Door to Liability," *Business Lexington*, March 19, 2009. http://bizlex.com.

As you read, consider the following questions:

1. As maintained by Masterton, what is behind a parent's idea of playing host to underage drinking parties for their children?
2. Why is it not enough to take car keys away from drinking teenagers, in Masterton's opinion?
3. What example does the author provide to support her assertion that homeowners insurance may not cover adults who serve alcohol to minors?

What can be done about underage drinking? The idea of playing host to gatherings that involve underage drinking as a means of controlling them has become more common, although often with devastating results. "Kids are going to drink anyway," some parents argue, "and I would rather know where my kids are, so I have them invite their friends over here and they party in the backyard. Of course, I make them throw their car keys into a basket, so I know they are safe."

But exactly how safe are the kids, or the condoning adults?

Before parents open their homes to underage drinking parties, it's important to consider the potential consequences, including the host's potential criminal liability, the host's potential civil liability, and most importantly, the danger to the kids.

Potential Criminal Liability

Parents who are hosting underage drinking parties are not helping their kids. They are breaking the law.

It is hard to imagine that any adults do not know that it is illegal to provide alcoholic beverages to kids, considering that there are signs in every liquor store. But apparently people are ignoring the very real possibility of prosecution for allowing drinking parties in their homes.

In Kentucky, a person is "guilty of unlawful transaction with a minor . . . if he knowingly sells, gives, purchases or procures any alcoholic or malt beverage in any form to or for a minor."

Also, "No person shall aid or assist any person under 21 years of age in purchasing or having delivered or served to him or her any alcoholic beverages."

According to Lee Turpin, director of litigation for the Fayette County attorney's office, hosts need to understand that they can be criminally charged under these statutes. The charges are Class A misdemeanors; if convicted the hosts face penalties of up to 12 months in jail and a $500 fine for each occurrence. For the first offense, they probably would wind up with probation, but, depending on the circumstances, there could be some jail time. Turpin said, "There is no standard offer for that offense, but it would not be just a fine." She also cautioned that the Cabinet for Health and Family Services could be involved; in the most extreme case, the children might be removed from the parents' care.

According to a recent CNN article entitled "Teen Drinking Leads to Crackdown on 'Cool' Parents," teen binge drinking is reaching epidemic proportions. There is a nationwide movement to enact "social hosting" laws, which would allow for hefty fines for people whose homes are venues for underage drinking parties; many of these laws hold the homeowners liable regardless of whether they knew about the parties. The MADD [Mothers Against Drunk Driving] website lists the states and communities which have enacted these laws, and the list is growing.

Potential Civil Liability

Don't people remember what it was like to be a teenager? It is simply not enough to take away the car keys. What about the kids who pass out? What if they drown in their vomit? What if they succumb to alcohol poisoning, and no one sees them

The Need for Social Host Laws

It's already illegal to sell or serve alcohol to minors. Why do we need social host laws?

In a party setting, it is often difficult or impossible to identify who provided the alcohol, and it makes more sense to assign responsibility to those who knew or should have known a drinking party was occurring on their property. Social host ordinances also have a deterrent effect, encouraging property owners to prevent such parties.

Mothers Against Drunk Driving, "Social Host," 2008. www.madd.org.

in time to get them to a hospital? And what about the kids who are so determined to drive that they find the extra set of keys, drive off, and cause a wreck? Or kill someone?

Do These People Really Want to Be Sued?

Currently, there is no social host liability in Kentucky, but a majority of states have social host liability in some form, and a recent Kentucky federal case forecasted that it is just a matter of time before we have it here. In *[Estate of] Vosnick v. RRJC, Inc.*, a 2002 case, Judge [Joseph M.] Hood predicted that "Kentucky would recognize a cause of action against social hosts . . . for serving alcohol to minors. . . ."

But that is what homeowners insurance is for, right? Not so fast.

According to a recent case from West Virginia, *American Modern Home Insurance Company v. [Jeff] Corra*, Corra gave a beer to one of his daughter's underage friends, who was later the driver in a fatal car accident. The families of the people who were killed sued Corra, but Corra's homeowners insurance company claimed that it did not have to defend or indemnify Corra. The West Virginia Supreme Court of Appeals agreed, saying that the policy language "does not provide coverage where the injury or damage is allegedly caused by the homeowner's conduct in knowingly permitting an underage adult to consume alcoholic beverages on the homeowner's property."

According to Mark Reed, a Lexington State Farm agent, this is an "insurance company's nightmare."

"The chances of something going wrong are not that far-fetched," he said. "If there is some problem, there are going to be lawsuits, and the party hosts are going to be dragged into that. Any time you get alcohol and injuries involved, there will be parents with vengeance on their minds. You've got a dead kid, a paralyzed kid. They would go after the party host's house and everything they could possibly get; it is not a matter of money anymore."

Before people think about hosting an underage drinking party, they should read their homeowners policy carefully. They just might find that hosting an underage drinking party is not worth risking their home.

Danger to the Kids

Finally, and most importantly, we should be thinking about the kids.

Some people believe that drinking parties are a rite of passage. Other parents condone drinking, relieved that their kids are not abusing the array of other drugs available to them, but those attitudes ignore the real picture. Alcohol abuse is as harmful as any of the scarier choices kids can make; it is not safe for kids to be at drinking parties. . . .

According to the MADD website, "There is a strong correlation between youth alcohol use and violence, risky sexual behavior, poor school performance, and even suicide."

So parents need to protect their kids. Parenting is not a popularity contest to see who is the "coolest" parent. It really is all right to say no.

Periodical and Internet Sources Bibliography

The following articles have been selected to supplement the diverse views presented in this chapter.

Linda Carroll	"Letting Teen Drink Under Parent's Watch Backfires," MSNBC.com, April 29, 2011.
Jason Lundberg	"Parental Liability for the Acts of a Minor Child," EzineArticles.com, March 15, 2010.
Robert McCoppin	"Ruling on Teen Parties Raises Questions Among Parents," *Chicago Tribune*, May 30, 2011.
New Media Rights	"Are Parents Liable for Children's Illegal File-sharing?," November 16, 2011. www.newmediarights.org.
Carl Pickhardt	"Adolescence and the Limits of Parental Responsibility," *Surviving (Your Child's) Adolescence* (blog), *Psychology Today*, October 18, 2009.
David Sack	"Why Being the 'Cool Parent' Isn't So Cool," PsychCentral.com, March 6, 2012.
Richard Weissbourd and Stephanie M. Jones	"Preventing Bullying Begins with Us," *Huffington Post*, February 28, 2012.
David Ziemer	"Liability for Teen Drinking Party Denied," *Wisconsin Law Journal*, March 2008.

For Further Discussion

Chapter 1

1. James Dobson insists that corporal punishment can prevent confrontations between parents and children from escalating and is the most effective way to change children's unwanted attitudes. Melanie Barwick agrees that it results in immediate compliance, but that it does not teach children to internalize good behavior. In your opinion, who has the stronger position? Use examples from the viewpoints to support your response.
2. Doriane Lambelet Coleman, Kenneth A. Dodge, and Sarah Keeton Campbell propose a legal definition separating punishment and abuse based on the presence of functional physical impairment. In your opinion, is their definition more accurate than the current ones they describe? Cite examples from the texts to explain your answer.
3. Ennio Cipani proposes that punishments fail when parents assume that the child is resistant to it and discontinue discipline. On the other hand, Tara Parker-Pope maintains that punishment is a form of negative reinforcement that teaches children that misbehavior attracts attention. In your view, which author offers the more compelling explanation? Explain your reasoning.

Chapter 2

1. Deborrah Cooper contends that young single parents are unprepared financially and emotionally to care for a child. However, Sabrina Broadbent asserts that parents who stay together for a child can create a more desperate situation for themselves later in life if they delay having a career to care for their young children. In your opinion, who pre-

sents the more persuasive argument? Use examples from the viewpoints to support your response.

2. George W. Dent Jr. argues that homosexual parenting is disadvantageous because of the fragility and promiscuity of same-sex relationships. In contrast, Stephanie Pappas insists that same-sex couples are superior parents because strong commitment is necessary for them to adopt or have children. In your opinion, which author has the more credible stance? Cite examples from the texts to explain your answer.
3. Lauren Sandler states that the distress felt by children living in cohabiting households is caused by stereotypes and misperceptions of unmarried parents. In your view, does the Institute for American Values perpetuate any stereotypes about cohabiting parents? Use examples from the viewpoints to support your response.

Chapter 3

1. Steve Mayes gives several examples of failures in laws requiring monetary compensation for victims of juvenile crimes. Cite examples from the texts and explain what can be done to make some parental financial liability laws more effective.
2. Melinda Beck points out that some parents believe serving alcohol to children under their supervision will help their teenagers drink responsibly as adults. In your view, do the potential liabilities described by Lucinda Masterton outweigh the supposed benefits of this practice? Why or why not?

Organizations to Contact

The editors have compiled the following list of organizations concerned with the issues debated in this book. The descriptions are derived from materials provided by the organizations. All have publications or information available for interested readers. The list was compiled on the date of publication of the present volume; the information provided here may change. Be aware that many organizations take several weeks or longer to respond to inquiries, so allow as much time as possible.

American Civil Liberties Union (ACLU)
125 Broad Street, 18th Floor, New York, NY 10004
(212) 549-2500
e-mail: infoaclu@aclu.org
website: www.aclu.org

The American Civil Liberties Union (ACLU) is a national organization that works to defend the rights guaranteed by the US Constitution. Its primary work is to support court cases against government actions that violate these rights. The ACLU publishes and distributes numerous policy statements, including those regarding laws on same-sex adoption by state, and reports, including "Too High a Price: The Case Against Restricting Gay Parenting."

Cato Institute
1000 Massachusetts Avenue NW
Washington, DC 20001-5403
(202) 842-0200 • fax: (202) 842-3490
website: www.cato.org

The Cato Institute is a public policy research foundation dedicated to limiting the role of government, protecting individual liberties, and promoting free markets. The institute commissions a variety of publications, including books, monographs, briefing papers, and other studies. Among its publications are the quarterly magazine *Regulation*, the bimonthly *Cato Policy Report*, and numerous articles on single parents and marriage.

Concerned Women for America (CWA)
1015 Fifteenth Street NW, Suite 1100, Washington, DC 20005
(202) 488-7000 • fax: (202) 488-0806
e-mail: mail@cwfa.org
website: www.cwfa.org

Concerned Women for America (CWA) is a public policy women's organization that has the goal of bringing biblical principles into all levels of public policy. CWA focuses on six core issues—family, sanctity of human life, education, pornography, religious liberty, and national sovereignty—through prayer, education, and social influence. The organization's brochures, fact sheets, and articles available on its website cover definitions of the family.

Focus on the Family
Colorado Springs, CO 80995
website: www.focusonthefamily.com

Focus on the Family is a Christian organization that works to nurture and defend what it views as the God-ordained institution of the family. The organization works to promote the permanence of marriage, the sanctity of human life, and the value of male and female sexuality. Among the many publications on parenting the organization produces are the articles "The Wonders of Reality Discpline" and "The Value of Stay-at-Home Moms."

Human Rights Campaign (HRC)
1640 Rhode Island Avenue NW, Washington, DC 20036-3278
(202) 628-4160 • fax: (202) 347-5323
website: www.hrc.org

Human Rights Campaign (HRC) is America's largest civil rights organization working to achieve gay, lesbian, bisexual, and transgender (GLBT) equality. The campaign works to secure equal rights for GLBT individuals at the federal and state levels by lobbying elected officials and mobilizing grassroots supporters. On its website, HRC offers information that surveys the issues of adoption, foster parenting, and GLBT families.

Legal Momentum

395 Hudson Street, New York, NY 10014
(212) 925-6635
website: www.legalmomentum.org

Legal Momentum is the nation's oldest legal defense and education fund dedicated to advancing the rights of all women and girls. Legal Momentum works to advance these rights through litigation and public policy advocacy to secure economic and personal security for women. Its reports on single motherhood cover issues such as poverty, government assistance, employment, and economics.

National Coalition for Men (NCFM)

932 C Street, Suite B, San Diego, CA 92101
(619) 231-1909
e-mail: ncfm@ncfm.org
website: www.ncfm.org

The National Coalition for Men (NCFM) is a nonprofit educational organization committed to ending sex discrimination. The coalition works to raise awareness about the ways sex discrimination affects men and boys. NCFM's website provides information on issues such as fatherhood and men's reproductive rights.

National Foster Parent Association (NFPA)

2021 E. Hennepin Avenue, Suite 320
Minneapolis, MN 55413-1769
(800) 557-5238 • fax: (888) 925-5634
e-mail: info@nfpaonline.org
website: www.nfpainc.org

Founded in 1972, the National Foster Parent Association (NFPA) advocates for the thousands of families that foster more than four hundred thousand children in out-of-home placement in the United States. The association's goal is to support foster parents in achieving safety, permanence, and well-being for the children and youth in its care. It publishes newsletters and provides resources on statutes and tax policies for foster parenting.

National Organization for Women (NOW)
1100 H Street NW, Suite 300, Washington, DC 20005
(202) 628-8669
website: www.now.org

The National Organization for Women (NOW) is the largest organization of feminist activists in the United States working to take action to bring about equality for all women. It works to eliminate discrimination and harassment in the workplace, schools, the justice system, and all other sectors of society; secure abortion, birth control, and reproductive rights for all women; end all forms of violence against women; eradicate racism, sexism, and homophobia; and promote equality and justice in our society. NOW has many publications available at its website, including the article "Caregiving Is a Feminist Issue."

Single Parent Advocate
e-mail: info@singleparentadvocate.org
website: http://singleparentadvocate.org

Single Parent Advocate is a nonprofit organization committed to educating, equipping, and empowering single parents with resources, practical assistance, emotional encouragement, and social networking to better their lives and the lives of their children. Its website offers a "Get Advice" section featuring articles contributed by counselors.

Bibliography of Books

Naomi Aldort — *Raising Our Children, Raising Ourselves*. Bothell, WA: Book Publishers Network, 2009.

Elisabeth Badinter — *The Conflict: How Modern Motherhood Undermines the Status of Women*. New York: Metropolitan Books/Henry Holt and Co., 2011.

Carlos Ball — *The Right to Be Parents: LGBT Families and the Transformation of Parenthood*. New York: New York University Press, 2012.

Lawrence J. Cohen — *Playful Parenting: A Bold New Way to Nurture Close Connections, Solve Behavior Problems, and Encourage Children's Confidence*. New York: Ballantine Books, 2001.

Pamela Druckerman — *Bringing Up Bébé: One American Mother Discovers the Wisdom of French Parenting*. New York: Penguin Press, 2012.

Rachel Gathercole — *The Well-Adjusted Child: The Social Benefits of Homeschooling*. Denver, CO: Mapletree Publishing Co., 2007.

Rosanna Hertz — *Single by Chance, Mothers by Choice: How Women Are Choosing Parenthood Without Marriage and Creating the New American Family*. New York: Oxford University Press, 2006.

Tom Hodgkinson	*The Idle Parent: Why Laid-Back Parents Raise Happier and Healthier Kids*. New York: Penguin, 2010.
Saul D. Hoffman and Rebecca A Maynard, eds.	*Kids Having Kids: Economic Costs & Social Consequences of Teen Pregnancy*. 2nd ed. Washington, DC: Urban Institute Press, 2008.
Carl Honoré	*Under Pressure: Rescuing Our Children from the Culture of Hyper-Parenting*. New York: HarperOne, 2008.
Mei-Ling Hopgood	*How Eskimos Keep Their Babies Warm: And Other Adventures in Parenting (From Argentina to Tanzania and Everywhere In Between)*. Chapel Hill, NC: Algonquin Books of Chapel Hill, 2012.
Dan Kindlon	*Too Much of a Good Thing: Raising Children of Character in an Indulgent Age*. New York: Hyperion, 2001.
Alfie Kohn	*Unconditional Parenting: Moving from Rewards and Punishments to Love and Reason*. New York: Atria Books, 2006.
Madeline Levine	*The Price of Privilege: How Parental Pressure and Material Advantage Are Creating a Generation of Disconnected and Unhappy Kids*. New York: HarperCollins, 2006.

Hara Estroff Marano	*A Nation of Wimps: The High Cost of Invasive Parenting*. New York: Broadway Books, 2008.
Donald Miller	*Father Fiction: Chapters for a Fatherless Generation*. Nashville, TN: Howard Books, 2010.
Gordon Neufeld and Gabor Maté	*Hold On to Your Kids: Why Parents Need to Matter More than Peers*. New York: Ballantine Books, 2005.
Kim John Payne with Lisa M. Ross	*Simplicity Parenting: Using the Extraordinary Power of Less to Raise Calmer, Happier, and More Secure Kids*. New York: Ballantine Books, 2009.
Adam Pertman	*Adoption Nation: How the Adoption Revolution Is Transforming Our Families—and America*. 2nd ed. Boston, MA: Harvard Common Press, 2011.
Norvin Richards	*The Ethics of Parenthood*. New York: Oxford University Press, 2010.
Meredith F. Small	*Kids: How Biology and Culture Shape the Way We Raise Our Children*. New York: Doubleday, 2001.
John Sowers	*Fatherless Generation: Redeeming the Story*. Grand Rapids, MI: Zondervan, 2010.
Dawn Stefanowicz	*Out from Under: The Impact of Homosexual Parenting*. Enumclaw, WA: Annotation Press, 2007.

Zach Wahls with Bruce Littlefield — *My Two Moms: Lessons of Love, Strength, and What Makes a Family.* New York: Gotham Books, 2012.

Richard Weissbourd — *The Parents We Mean to Be: How Well-Intentioned Adults Undermine Children's Moral and Emotional Development.* Boston, MA: Houghton Mifflin Harcourt, 2009.

Index

A

B

C

D

E

F

G

H

I

J

K

Q

R

S

CPSIA information can be obtained
at www.ICGtesting.com
Printed in the USA
FFOW021103180213